Yale Language Series

EDITED BY PETER C. PATRIKIS

Reading Between the Lines

PERSPECTIVES ON FOREIGN

LANGUAGE LITERACY

Yale University Press

New Haven &

London

Publisher: Mary Jane Peluso
Editorial Assistant: Emily Saglimbeni
Manuscript Editor: Jane Zanichkowsky
Production Editor: Margaret Otzel
Marketing Coordinator: Tim Shea
Production Coordinator: Joyce Ippolito

Set in Minion type by Keystone Typesetting, Inc.
Printed in the United States of America.

Library of Congress Cataloging-in-Publication Data
Reading between the lines : perspectives on foreign language literacy /
edited by Peter C. Patrikis.
p. cm. — (Yale language series)
Includes bibliographical references and index.
ISBN 0-300-09781-6 (pbk. : alk. paper)
1. Language and languages—Study and teaching. 2. Literacy—Study and teaching.
I. Patrikis, Peter Charles. II. Series.
P53.475 .R43 2003
418'.0071—dc21
2002033171

A catalogue record for this book is available from the British Library.

10   9   8   7   6   5   4   3   2   1

. . . et femina dux erat

To Claire Kramsch
for leading the way

Contents

Preface

The essays in this volume were originally presented at two conferences conducted by the Consortium for Language Teaching and Learning: one on technology, foreign languages, and undergraduate education held at the Massachusetts Institute of Technology in October 1998, the other on new perspectives on foreign language literacy held at Brown University in October 2000. That these essays, all of which have been extensively revised, are gathered in one volume is not mere serendipity: the chapters share a renewed emphasis on reading in the teaching and learning of foreign languages.

I am grateful to the contributors for their willingness to include their essays here and for their patience on the long road from conference to book. And I am grateful to the readers of the earlier draft of the collection: Mary Ann MacDonald Carolan of Fairfield University, David Goldberg of the Association of Departments of Foreign Languages, and especially James S. Noblitt of the University of North Carolina at Chapel Hill, whose guidance, wit, common sense, wisdom, generosity, and friendship I treasure.

Finally, I would like to express my thanks to the Andrew W. Mellon Foundation and the C. V. Starr Foundation for their generous and enlightened support of the Consortium's conferences.

Introduction

PETER C. PATRIKIS

Only in the stream of thought and life do words have meaning.
—Ludwig Wittgenstein

It is then that the reader asks that crucial question, "What's it all about?" But the what "it" is, is not the actual text . . . but the text the reader has constructed under its sway.
—Jerome Bruner

Between the lines . . . The titular metaphor of this book has an admittedly Zen-like or postmodern character. It suggests presence by absence, meaning where nothing is written, a third or higher dimension hidden from the view of those who inhabit Flatland. At the same time, it is a simple and common metaphor that affirms that every text is more than the sum of its parts, that every text means more than the linear assembly of its individual words, their dictionary definitions, their morphology or structure, and their syntactic relations with other words. A text does more than realize linguistic code in context. It also refers back to other texts, what Henry Widdowson, borrowing a term from literary theory, has called "intertextuality" (Widdowson 1992). An invitation to a wedding, a memorandum announcing a staff meeting, a letter of complaint about a defective purchase—such texts, and they are of course innumerable, embody social and cultural norms, and those norms are actualized with reference to previous texts. Citation, allusion, patterns of rhetorical organization, and genre protocols assume routine and predictable forms. We do not speak and write with complete originality. When we speak and write, we place ourselves in a textual tradition of expectation and authorization. We play with that tradition (we should recall that the Latin root of the word *allude* means "to play"), but we do not violate it. Such violation might be ignorance of the rules. It might be idiocy (the Greek root of that word—ιδιοτ—suggests a private language). Or it might be lyric poetry, when we consider the examples of Mallarmé, a Celan, or one of the Surrealists. In other words, language learning has not only a social and cultural dimension but also a *historical* dimension. A text must reach into the past in order to be comprehensible, as I have discussed in an essay on culture and language teaching (Patrikis 2000).

Every teacher of language will recognize in the metaphor of reading between the lines the primordial difficulty of every student: to move beyond token-for-token processing to analysis and the understanding of the multiple meanings of a text, to progress from mere decoding to rich interpretation. And every teacher will recognize that trivial texts are not effective in guiding students to higher levels of reading.

The neglect of serious reading—by which I mean reading that does more than hunt for facts, that is more than referential, that provokes questions, that awakens the judgment and imagination—took hold in the heyday of the oral proficiency movement with its reaction against the supposedly rebarbative practices of the grammar translation movement and with its putatively pragmatic approach to oral communication in reaction against the limitations of the AudioLingual Method. Signs in train stations and weather reports passed for significant texts, readily decipherable by the novice learner. Poetry was largely consigned to the dustbin, as Carl Blyth notes in his chapter with regard to a poem by Jacques Prévert. Similarly, the perplexities of cross-cultural encounters evaporated in the bland give-and-take of question and answer in short interviews. The widespread demise of serious reading reflected the baby-with-the-bathwater mentality that often appears to characterize what is seen as progress in the teaching and learning of foreign languages.

What takes place within the field of foreign languages mirrors what takes place in the wider economic, political, and social culture, as two major retrospective surveys have demonstrated (Kramsch and Kramsch 2000; Lantolf and Sunderman 2001). For many years now, and with increasing frequency, we have come across repeated announcements of the death of reading (for example, Highfield 2000; Johnson 1995): television, computer games, Web surfing, and almost any other form of entertainment have been invariably invoked and condemned as lethal to the life of the mind and inimical to the permanence of the written word. (These arguments follow in the lineage of Plato's criticism of poetry.) No one has argued the case more ardently and more elegantly than the distinguished and eccentric literary critic Harold Bloom. In an interview published in the *Yale Bulletin and Calendar* (2000) following the publication of his book *How to Read and Why,* Bloom lamented, "The real enemy [of reading] now is the screen. Whether it's the TV screen or the motion picture screen or most likely, in the end, the computer screen. The real enemy is the Internet." A similar sentiment issues from Esther Dyson, computer guru and member of President Clinton's advisory board on the National Information Infrastructure. In her book *Release 2.0* Dyson frets about whether the world of multimedia is undermining the reading of texts (Dyson 1997). If in the past we were accustomed to debating the relation of orality and literacy, we now seem to have shifted the terms of the argument to literacy and multimedia. In his essay William A. Johnson traces the evolution of the distinction.

In sharp contradistinction to Bloom's apocalyptic pronouncement about literacy, many foreign language classes and many of the essays in this volume testify to a renewed interest in reading, which is in fact promoted and not diminished by the World Wide Web. Anecdotes and examples abound.

In a presentation to a group of visiting language teachers Andrée Grandjean-Levy of Cornell University discussed an intermediate French course that was based almost exclusively on Web sites in France. One day she witnessed a student struggling alone at the computer through a difficult, complex text about an elegant restaurant in Brittany, the kind of purple touristic prose that in the past would have been unimaginable and deemed impossible at the intermediate level. The student read with great concentration and at the end of the passage exclaimed aloud to himself in English, "Wow! That's cool!"

During a site visit to a liberal arts college in New England, a German teacher recounted to me that his analogous Web-based experiment with an intermediate course on Berlin had surprising results: the students did much more work, much better work, much more independent work, much more creative work, and declared that it was their favorite course. These anecdotes suggest that students want to read real texts from the real world, that they are willing to make the effort to do more when they are intellectually motivated, and that the World Wide Web abolishes dogmatic distinctions among elementary, intermediate, and advanced texts. The anecdotes suggest—and dozens of colleagues have confirmed—that students are motivated by virtual texts, whereas they are nonplussed by the same texts in a textbook. What is interesting and has yet to be adequately explained, is that even remarkable texts seem deadened by marginal notations, by established agendas (known as "pre-reading" and "post-reading"), and by often numbingly transparent questions that serve no purpose other than "checking comprehension."

The renewed emphasis on reading in foreign languages has other sources unrelated to the hyperbolic library of the World Wide Web: (1) the expansion of the traditional foreign language classroom beyond its four closed walls to include written communication with students, teachers, and other individuals across the globe (see Furstenberg in this volume; Kern 1996; and Koike 1998); (2) the movement to promote foreign languages across the curriculum (Krueger and Ryan 1993); and (3) an increasing dissatisfaction with narrowly defined notions of oral proficiency (Roche and Salumets 1996).

The strongest impetus for renewing the importance of reading is perhaps the reconsideration of the role of foreign languages in undergraduate liberal education. As colleagues across the country rethink the place of foreign languages in the undergraduate curriculum, they are confirming that place as a fundamental aspect of general education and consequently reasserting the importance of reading and interpreting a text. The humanistic rationale for the study of foreign languages has been as persistent (see Lantolf and Sunderman 2001, pp. 8–11). That rationale has also been consistently wishy-washy. Assertions of the value of foreign languages

- the study of foreign language disciplines the mind
- the study of foreign languages teaches about one's native language
- the study of foreign languages promotes understanding of "the other"

ring hollow, not because they are incorrect—they are not!—but because they have become platitudinous pieties and because these values seldom seem to have any concrete realization or practical reflection in the actual foreign language classroom. These assertions have attained the status of axioms, when in fact they are hypotheses requiring demonstration and proof, so that students, teachers, parents, professors of literature, administrators, accreditation boards, and trustees understand the goals and activities of foreign language study and also so that foreign language teachers remain vigilant in justifying the values of their courses and in actualizing those values in all aspects of their teaching. Patricia Chaput provides a radical rethinking of the values of undergraduate foreign language study in her forthcoming book on college language teaching.

The practical and educational values of foreign language study and of reading a foreign language text are not difficult to enumerate: close analysis of a text involves assembling facts, making contrasts and comparisons, understanding conventions, confronting differences, problem-solving, testing—indeed, challenging—assumptions, constructing hypotheses, making informed judgments . . . in short, reading between the lines.

The subject of reading is by no means a novel one in the field of foreign languages, and it has captured the attention of many scholars (for two examples, see Kramsch 1993; Swaffar, Arens, and Byrnes 1991). This volume seeks to strike out in other directions. The space between the lines of a text is capacious and deep, so it does not come as a surprise that the contributors to this volume enter that space in different ways and with different perspectives. Each chapter is an invitation to a new perspective, and collectively the essays suggest the richness and difference of many new ways of considering the acts of reading and interpreting texts and cultures. Oddly, in the past, reading often has been characterized as a *passive* skill, as if the words on the page or screen simply had to be absorbed and processed. All the authors presented in this volume understand and advocate an activist approach. They represent a variety of languages—English, Czech, French, German, Greek, Japanese, Latin, and Spanish—and an even greater variety of perspectives, including cognitive theory, critical applied linguistics, technology as hermeneutic, history, literary theory, and cross-cultural analysis. Yet all concur in their understanding that reading is a cultural initiation and a cultural practice that lies at the heart of humanistic inquiry.

William A. Johnson opens the collection by turning the tables on many conventional notions about literacy and common theories about reading and technology: insisting that reading is a social rather than an individual or even isolating activity, he adumbrates the concept of a "reading culture," while exploring the technologies of that culture both in Greco-Roman antiquity and in our computerized present. Literally examining the shape and size of the written line, Johnson looks between the lines to locate the sociocultural dynamics of reading culture and of the pedagogical culture of higher education.

Traversing cognitive science and hermeneutics, Mark Turner emphasizes the processes of conceptual blending as the fundamental differences between languages and cultures and suggests that adult learners of foreign languages should engage in specific comparisons of grammars and styles (learning how to blend templates). Turner looks between the lines to indicate that literacy is not displayed in surface features but resides in the ability to harmonize (blend, in his terms) features that conflict in order to make powerful inferences about the empty spaces between languages, and to forge conceptual integrations.

Presenting a magisterial overview of the scholarship on literacy, Richard G. Kern redefines literacy in order to propose a new model of classroom-based foreign language study. Building on what we might call the sociocultural turn in language teaching, Kern emphasizes the importance of critical reflection *as a learning device* and not simply as a political-educational stance. Reading is not merely a basic skill; it is the fundamental activity for creating, interpreting, and reflecting on meaning.

Attacking many of the shibboleths of current pedagogical orthodoxy, Carl Blyth argues that many contemporary methodologies impoverish the nature of language; he urges an approach that embraces the poetic and phatic functions of language and that restores pleasure to the foreign language curriculum. Blyth's call for attending to the aesthetic nature of language is echoed in the chapters by Furstenberg, Johnson, Kern, and Emde and Schneider, and it reflects his concern that the contemporary communicative approach fails to recognize the richness of language between the lines.

Analyzing massive amounts of data from on-line cross-cultural exchanges in English and French, Gilberte Furstenberg demonstrates how close reading, aided by modern information technology, leads to high-level investigation of cultural assumptions and to cross-cultural understanding. Although Furstenberg is aiming at developing cultural literacy, it is important to note how much that process and goal depend on reading, rereading, and reflecting on how others (fellow students in one class in the United States and fellow students in France) are reading and rereading. For her, reading between the lines is reading between the cultures.

With examples drawn from political discourse in Czech, English, and Japanese, Masako Ueda Fidler moves between the micro-level features of discourse analysis to macro-level features of cultural context to demonstrate that no one-sided approach can account for the many meanings of a text. Hers is one of the many endorsements in this volume of the notion that computer technology provides us with the means to enable students to discover those meanings on their own.

Exploiting a computer game technology in order to enhance reading and writing in an intermediate-level German language course, Silke von der Emde and Jeffrey Schneider merge play (the game) with work (language learning), postmodern literary theory with second language acquisition research, and self-reflection with communication to study another example of a reading culture. Between the lines they site—and catch sight of—possibilities of intellectual collaboration, critical engagement, and self-reflection. Like Furstenberg's, their students come to value rereading, what the authors call circular reading.

In his examination of teaching Franz Kafka, Mark Webber offers many double readings: reading in English and in German, interpretations in English and in German, educational readings of literature in translation and political readings of literature in translation. Between the lines and between the languages, Webber envisions translation (in its multiple senses) as yet another path to critical thinking and self-reflection.

Finally, Nicolas Shumway concludes the volume with a profound reminder that every choice made in the classroom is as much political and philosophical as it is pedagogical and heuristic, that teaching foreign language literacy is a moral as well as an educational responsibility. At a far remove from belletristic aestheticism, Shumway's notion of reading between the lines erases the bland neutrality of the foreign language syllabus and pushes teachers and students alike to the limits of the moral imagination.

It will not require a perceptive reader to identify many other commonalities among the contributions to this volume: technology at the service of teaching and learning; the changing role and decreasing significance of the all-purpose textbook; the shifting responsibilities of students and teachers; deep questioning of the current conventions of the foreign language profession; the creation of reading communities and of literate cultures within the classroom; and the restoration of foreign language study to the heart of the humanities. Little in this collection of essays suggests that the teaching of foreign languages is going to get any easier: new demands, new possibilities, new information, and new insights open the spaces between the lines ever wider.

References

Bloom Extols Pleasures of Solitary Reading. *Yale Bulletin and Calendar* 29(1) (September 1, 2000) ⟨http://www.yale.edu/opa/v29.n1/story4.html⟩.

Bloom, H. (2000). *How to Read and Why.* New York: Scribner.

Bruner, J. S. (1986). *Actual Minds, Possible Worlds.* Cambridge: Harvard University Press.

Chaput, P. (forthcoming). *College Language Teaching.* New Haven: Yale University Press.

Dyson, E. (1997). *Release 2.0: A Design for Living in the Digital Age.* New York: Broadway.

Furstenberg, G. (1997). Teaching with Technology: What Is at Stake? *ADFL Bulletin* 28(3): 21–25.

Highfield, R. (2000). Thinkers Forecast the End for Money and the Written Word (January 11, 2000) ⟨http://www.smh.com.au/news/0001/11/features/features4.html⟩.

Johnson, S. (1995). Repossession: An Academic Romance: The Rossetti Archive and the Quest to Revive Scholarly Editing. *Lingua Franca* 5(4) ⟨http://www.linguafranca.com/9505/repossession.html⟩.

Kern, R. (1996). Computer-Mediated Communication: Using E-Mail Exchanges to Explore Personal Histories in Two Cultures. In *Telecollaboration in Foreign Language*

Learning: Proceedings of the Hawaii Symposium, edited by M. Warschauer, pp. 105–19. Honolulu: University of Hawaii Second Language Teaching and Curriculum Center.

Koike, Y. (1998). Who Is Teaching My Students? Paper presented at the conference "Transformations: Computers, Foreign Languages, and Undergraduate Education," Massachusetts Institute of Technology, Cambridge, October 1998.

Kramsch, C. (1993). *Context and Culture in Language Teaching.* Oxford: Oxford University Press.

——, ed. (1995). *Redefining the Boundaries of Foreign Language Study.* AAUSC Issues in Language Program Direction. Boston: Heinle & Heinle.

Kramsch, C., and O. Kramsch. (2000). The Avatars of Literature in Language Study. *Modern Language Journal* 84(4): 553–73.

Krueger, M., and Ryan F., eds. (1993). *Language and Content: Discipline- and Content-Based Approaches to Language Study.* Heath Series on Foreign Language Acquisition Research and Instruction. Lexington, Mass.: Heath.

Lantolf, J. P., and G. Sunderman. (2001). The Struggle for a Place in the Sun: Rationalizing Foreign Language Study in the Twentieth Century. *Modern Language Journal* 85(1): 5–25.

Patrikis, P. C. (2000). Site Under Construction: The Web of Language, Culture, and Literacy. In *The Learning and Teaching of Slavic Languages and Cultures,* edited by O. Kagan and B. Rifkin, pp. 45–60. Bloomington, Ind.: Slavica.

Roche, J., and T. Salumets, eds. (1996). *Germanics Under Construction: Intercultural and Interdisciplinary Prospects.* Studium Deutsch als Fremdsprache—Sprachdidaktik, vol. 10. Munich: Iudicium Verlag.

Swaffar, J., K. M. Arens, and H. Byrnes. (1991). *Reading for Meaning: An Integrated Approach to Language Learning.* Englewood Cliffs, N.J.: Prentice-Hall.

Widdowson, H. (1992). The Relevant Conditions of Language Use and Learning. In *Language and Content: Discipline-Based Approaches to Language Study,* edited by Merle Krueger and Frank Ryan. Lexington, Mass.: Heath, 27–36.

Wittgenstein, L. (1981). *Zettel,* 2d. ed. Edited by G. E. M. Anscombe and G. H. V. Wright. Oxford: Blackwell.

1

Reading Cultures and Education

WILLIAM A. JOHNSON

In this essay I wish to invite reflection on reading or, more precisely, on reading culture. As a cultural historian and a classicist, I naturally want to ground my thoughts historically, and I propose to do so by means of contrapuntal sketches from the reading culture of classical antiquity. Indeed the reader will have to grant me some indulgence in rooting this set of reflections so particularly in my own deepest scholarly interest, which is the reading culture of the ancient Greeks. But I hope to convince you, first, that consideration of the "otherness" of an ancient reading culture can help to sharpen considerably our perspective on reading cultures generally—including our contemporary technologically driven one. Second, although most will readily grant a broad relation between reading and education, I hope also to convince you that the understanding of reading culture is central to perceiving in its particulars not only how technological change may affect education but also how educators, and in particular instructors in the humanities, may be able to derive clear advantage from technological change.

But what do I intend by speaking of reading as "reading culture"? Reading, I will insist, is a social rather than an individual phenomenon, one that develops over time, with deep roots in the traditions of a given society. Reading is not, in my view, an act, or even a process, but a *system,* a highly complex cultural system that involves a great many considerations beyond the decoding by the reader of the words of the (author's) text. I therefore speak deliberately of "reading culture" rather than of "literacy" or of "writing technologies," both because that is my preferred focus and because I think mistaken the sort of analysis that starts from the viewpoint either that writing is a watershed phenomenon, and thus the world divides into literate and nonliterate, or that writing is a "technology" that can be studied in isolation, as though the whole of reading were the interaction between the technology and the user of that technology. That reading involves many variables, that there are in fact many types of reading, that reading is a complex cultural system, may seem very obvious propositions. But these points have been so willfully neglected by such a long and distinguished line of researchers that I do not think they can be overemphasized here at the start of these reflections.

Indeed, what prompts me to this more general and theoretical consideration of reading culture is my deep dissatisfaction with the terms in which researchers have typically sought to describe both ancient and contemporary reading cultures. As I ponder these matters, I come increasingly to believe that the very missteps made in analysis of the ancient world, some of which are generally recognized as missteps today, are being repeated, *mutatis mutandis,* in contemporary commentary on the great paradigm shift going on about us, often called the "electronic revolution"—a central aspect of which is, in my view, a shift in the paradigm of the contemporary reading culture. As a cultural historian, I have come to hope, then, that a better understanding of how best to describe ancient reading culture may help as we seek to understand the changes in our own. But more detail on that after I have done a bit of historical mortar as background for this inquiry.

Some Typical Fallacies in the Analysis of Reading Culture

A prominent strategy in the analysis of reading culture has for a long while been a focus on literacy, usually opposed to the oral culture, or "orality," that literacy is said to replace. Much of the early debate on this subject concentrated, remarkably, on classical Athens, and one thinks in particular of that *annus mirabilis,* 1963, which saw seminal publications by the anthropologist Jack Goody ("The consequences of literacy," written with Ian Watt, a professor of English literature) and the classicist Eric Havelock (*Preface to Plato*). These scholars and their followers have presented a variety of formulations over the years, but in essence their mode of analysis seeks to establish a consequential relation between, on one hand, the so-called rise of rationalism in classical Athens and, on the other, the introduction of the alphabet and of literate modes of thought into the previously oral society. Because the use of writing leads to a self-consciousness about elements of the spoken language (Havelock 1963; compare Olson 1994), or because writing sets statements in a form in which the texts can be compared (Goody and Watt 1963, pp. 304–45), or because writing lends itself to different habits in the accumulation of information, such as the creation of lists (Goody 1977), writing is taken to be directly causative in the genesis of an analytic, critical frame of mind and thus causative of things like logical analysis and detailed proof. It is, then, this self-conscious mode of analysis that leads to the cataclysmic moment when (we are told) myth is replaced by history, rhetoric by logic and philosophy, magic by science—when by virtue of the "rise of rationalism" the traditional mythological way of looking at things is cast off in favor of the modern conception of the world. At the most speculative reach of this set of theories, the liberalizing effects of the new rationalist intellectualism are taken so far as to account for the rise of democracy.

The specific problems with these theories scarcely need rehearsing (see Thomas 1992, pp. 15–28). For one thing, it seems fairly obvious that, if literacy is in itself such a powerful agent, we might expect the effects in ancient Greece to show up outside of Athens and Ionia. In any case, detailed research into oral cultures has not been able to affirm the sort of clear-cut, essential differences posited between literate and oral societies (for example, Finnegan 1988). Likewise, cognitive psychologists (I think in particular of the classic 1981 study by Scribner and Coles, *The Psychology of Literacy*) have failed to find general cognitive differences in memory, classification, or logical abilities following the introduction of writing systems into an oral society.

Theories that rely on literacy as an agent of change are therefore not in good repute these days—but they continue to be enormously influential. Perhaps, then, it is worth a brief look at what is wrong, in methodological terms, about this sort of analysis. First is the easy misstep into technological determinism. Whether the focus has been on the alphabet, on literacy generally, or, as more recent and nuanced studies have done (see especially Olson 1994), on the technology of writing itself, there is a tendency to see cultural change as the immediate and indeed necessary result of the introduction of a technology. This reductionist tendency among researchers is hardly restricted to studies of ancient Greece. Amusingly similar conclusions about what "causes" the development of the modern conception of the world can be found, for instance, in Eisenstein's book on the printing press (Eisenstein 1979), and, most recently, in Saenger's account of how the introduction of spaces between words in medieval manuscripts led directly to the rise of complex, abstract thinking—this time in the twelfth century (Saenger 1997). In commentary on our era, a similar tendency presents itself. The computer is made the "cause" of a great many developments: loss of memory, loss of the ability to attend oral discourse, loss of expertise in reading. But, we ought to ask, in what sense is the introduction of technology directly causative?

The second methodological fallacy I would like to highlight is that of the replacement technology. In the orality-and-literacy debates I have just reviewed, a major problem has to do with the terms of the analysis. What is oral is seen as opposite to what is written. Thus oral society is taken to be opposite to literate society, and we coin a term, "orality," to oppose to "literacy." We can now say, although the meaning is not very clear, that literacy opposes orality and that as literacy rises, orality falls, that is, that literacy replaces orality. This may sound reasonable enough, in its vague way. But culture is not a zero-sum game. Scholars have spent a great deal of effort establishing exactly that: oral culture changes as literate culture is established and changes, but oral culture hardly goes away or even diminishes. Literacy and orality are simply not contrastive terms in any strict sense. (For striking medieval examples, see Carruthers 1990, and, more generally, Thomas 1992 and Finnegan 1988.)

Once again this sort of misstep is replaying itself in the contemporary debate. From Marshall McLuhan onwards, we encounter repeated suggestions that we are moving away from a fully literate era back to a "more oral" (or sometimes "more visual") society (McCluhan 1962). This sort of observation, which we now see to be problematic in itself, is often linked to predictions or anxieties about the demise of the printed book. In 1981, for example, I sat in a conference at UCLA in which the chair of the Classics Department confidently declared that the printed scholarly book would be unknown by the end of the decade and that new printed books of any type would soon be rare; more recently, in the *Times Literary Supplement* I read of the anxieties about what will happen as CD-ROMs (inevitably, it seems) replace printed books (Miller 1998, p. 7; compare Bolter 1991, pp. 1–3). But in contrast to the hype of the "paperless office" is the reality of offices awash in paper; in contrast to our anxieties about the demise of the book is the fact that more books are published and sold today than ever before. This is the replacement technology fallacy. The paradigm shift of the electronic revolution is often compared to sweeping changes brought on by the printing press and the automobile. We must be careful, however, about the terms of the analogy. The horseless carriage did replace the carriage with horse, and the printing press did replace the handwritten book. But electronic technology is not a replacement technology for printed materials in the same way. The automobile, after all, did not usher in a new age of proliferation of countless horses; nor did the printing press engender the production of numberless handwritten manuscripts. But the computer has accompanied an explosion in printed texts—alongside an explosion in digital texts. Likewise, in ancient Greece the use of writing and written records over time surely interacted with and helped change the use of oral discourse, but it did not obliterate it by any means and arguably did not diminish it. Written discourse is no more, for most purposes, a replacement technology for oral discourse than, for most purposes, CD-ROMs are a replacement technology for books.

The Sociocultural Construction of Reading

If we reject the sort of sweeping cultural analysis that charts movements from oral to literate and back to oral or onward to visual, or that focuses reductively on one part of the reading system, how then do we go about our analysis, and how does that analysis intersect with the topic announced in the title, namely, education? In analyzing the reading culture of the ancient Greeks, I seek to move from the known to the unknown, to see what differentiates reading in antiquity from the reading-from-a-printed-book model so familiar to us. As my work in this area has continued, I have found that the basis of analysis grows ever wider, for I must look not simply into cognitive models of how the reader interacts with the physical text but also at the physical setting of reading, the aesthetics of reading production and apprehension, the sociology of the groups participating in the reading—in broad terms, the *negotiated, sociocultural construction* of reading. In trying to understand what may be different about contemporary reading experiences in the new techno-culture, a similarly broad-based analysis seems to me essential. And—what makes the analysis important for the topic before us— as an educator, I am increasingly struck by how this broad-based analysis intersects materially both with problems in learning and with the sort of sociocultural dynamics that are central to the educational enterprise. Again, I take as my starting point an example from ancient Greece.

To begin, let us focus on how the physical tool, in ancient terms the book roll, interacts with our understanding of the system of reading. It will help simplify matters if we focus on a subset of ancient reading culture, so I will restrict my remarks to literary prose texts. Now, the ancient literary book is striking in several respects. (For full details on the ancient book, see Turner 1987; Johnson 2003.) The sort of book I have in mind is, of course, not a bound, printed volume but a handwritten roll, held horizontally, written in columns that were regular, left- and right-justified, and very narrow (about fifteen to twenty-five letters, that is, two to three inches, in width, and six to ten inches in height). The letters of the text were clearly, often calligraphically, written, but otherwise undifferentiated: that is, there were no spaces between words. The main sentence breaks were marked by a horizontal stroke at the left edge of the column, but there was otherwise little or no punctuation. And nothing to mark larger structures: no paragraph breaks, no running heads, no page or column numbers. The lines were divided rationally, at the end of a word or syllable, but otherwise the column was organized as a tight phalanx of clear, distinct letters, each marching one after the other to form an impression of continuous flow, the letters forming a solid rectangle of written text alternating with narrower bands of white space. The visual effect was, then, not unlike a strip of 35 mm film. The product seems, to the modern eye, something almost more akin to an art object than a book; and, with its lack of word spaces and punctuation, the ancient book roll seems spectacularly, even bewilderingly, impractical and inefficient as a reading tool.

This may seem an exceedingly strange way of putting together a book. But it was no flash in the pan. This idea of the literary book prevailed for almost one thousand years in the Greek tradition and was eventually adopted by the Romans in the early empire. How do we account for this type of book within the context of a stable and sophisticated reading culture? How is it that the Greeks were unable for so many centuries to adopt such obviously useful aids as word spaces, punctuation, paragraphing, and the like in their literary texts? Surprising as it may seem, the conclusion is hard to avoid that there was something about the reading culture that felt no need for these things, that in terms of the total system of reading, such habits as omitting spaces between words worked, and worked well. We cannot suppose that the Greeks were too naïve or primitive or stupid to think of word spaces or punctuation or structural markers. In ancient elementary school exercises, word division and punctuation are often found (Cribiore 1996). Ancient documentary texts often have elaborate visual structural markers, as needed. In the earliest Roman texts, word separation is the norm; in fact it is universal so far as we know (Wingo 1972), and it is telling that the Romans in imperial times *chose to discard word spaces* in the writing of their literary manuscripts, a choice they would hardly have made if it interfered fundamentally with their reading system. Such a development today—the discarding of spaces between words—is simply inconceivable. We see clearly, then, that there is something essentially different about the ancient reading system, that the *paradigm of reading* was different.

Defining the Difference: A New Paradigm of Reading

How do we define this difference in the paradigm of reading? Without going into too much detail, I will summarize briefly a few ways in which I approach the definition of the paradigm for ancient reading, because it is important as model and background to defining the paradigm shift in our own reading culture. One model I use is the cognitive one. I find, for instance, very interesting and probably significant that the extremely narrow column of text in an ancient book matches the amount of data that we tend to pre-process as we read. Our eye, as it reads, takes in chunks of about fifteen to twenty characters beyond the point of acute focus, and our brain uses this advance data for preliminary "decoding" of the script—and indeed fifteen to twenty characters is also how far ahead the eye typically keeps in front of the text as we are reading aloud (Saenger 1997, pp. 1–17 and bibliography). To this compare the fifteen to twenty letters that constitute the width of a prose column in an ancient book roll (Johnson 2003, pp. 167–77). We find, then, at least one possible reason why the lack of word spaces in literary texts did not seem to bother readers in antiquity: the text was already broken up into sufficiently digestible chunks by the narrow column widths. But this sort of technical observation is of limited use in and of itself and must be combined with other ways in which ancient reading differentiates itself if we are to make sense of the *reading culture.* The strangeness of the book roll intersects with the fact that literary texts were commonly "read" in the sense of a small group listening to a "performance" (as it were) by a lector (often a slave trained for this very purpose). Thus a performer, in effect, was usually interpreting the text, and the sort of direction for pause and tone given by the author's punctuation in our texts was left to the reader's "professional" interpretation of the lines. We need also to consider the fact that ancient literary books were hardly ever consulted in part or for reference. Thus the need for a text with clear structural markers did not exist. We might note, finally, that the very act of the calligraphic and expensive book being read to a group of the educated elite acted as a symbol of what bonded and validated the group as Greek, educated, cultured. That is, the physical aspect of the book, *taken as an element in the reading system as a whole,* seems to make sense in its own terms.

How, then, do we turn this sort of analysis around and use it in the understanding of reading today and in particular for our understanding of reading in an electronic environment? My first step is hesitating, unsure, treading well beyond my expertise. But it seems widely assumed in cognitive studies that the experiences of reading in an electronic environment and from a printed text are essentially the same. In fact, computer-controlled reading experiments form the backbone of a certain thread of research in cognitive psychology. Of course many parameters must be approximately equivalent, such as the way in which the eye in reading lines of text jumps at intervals across the page or virtual page ("the saccadic movement") or the amount of text on the periphery of the point of acute focus that the eye is able to take in. Yet computer screens are visually complex in a way that the printed page is not (Bolter 1991, p. 11), and reading on a computer screen seems, to me at least, cognitively somewhat different. Most computer users, for example, rarely read long, continuous text from a computer screen. Why is that? I for one would like to know a great deal more about how the interactions with the electronic interface do or do not affect the mechanics of the reading experience, that is, to what extent reading within the context of a hypertextually linked environment, a multiple-tasking environment, or an environment with a heavy emphasis on icons in lieu of text changes the very way in which our eyes move about and attempt to read the virtual page in front of us.

Cognitive studies of such matters are (so far as I have been able to find) mostly lacking, but even as we mark this down as a *desideratum,* we have already come to recognize that the cognitive model will be but one facet of the complex reading system I seek to describe. Even in the context of the physical (or virtual) printed text, cognitive models will only get us so far. In the discussion of the way in which the ancient physical text interacted with the system of reading, we found at once that it was necessary to discuss not simply the way in which the reader cognitively processed the narrow columns of letters without word division. We needed also to think about how the physical features of the text, not simply lack of word division but lack of punctuation or structural markers, interacted with the demands made on the text—as for example the fact that the text was read aloud by a trained reader and the fact that the text was not used for reference. This striking contrast, the utterly undifferentiated unstructuredness of the ancient physical text, suggests, by virtue of its radical difference, what seems to me the most characteristic feature of the contemporary reading experience. Our habit of reading is so different that we find it hard even to imagine a reading system that lacks physical structural markers, whether at the level of sentence, paragraph, or chapter. Essential to our own idea of reading is detailed, authorially controlled structure.

I will go further: there seems today to be an increasingly radical focus on the structural components of texts, and in many ways it is exactly the prominence of these structural features, or what I will call *navigational aids,* that in some ways strikes at the core of the contemporary reading culture. I highlight this feature because the strong presence of navigational aids seems to me not simply characteristic of contemporary texts but fundamental to many contemporary reading experiences. That the Internet is often cruised by Netscape Navigator™ is no coincidence in the metaphor I am proffering: it seems quintessential to much reading today that we are "browsing," that is, looking over a huge amount of written data in order to digest the information, or, more commonly, to find among the deluge of data the information we seek. This habit of information seeking is, I think, profound. But let me emphasize, again, that the computer does not cause it. In classical scholarship we find that the elaboration of structure and indices designed to facilitate information retrieval first became prominent in German texts of the end of the nineteenth century. It is simply that the electronic media are particularly well adapted to this sort of reading habit and in turn promote exactly these habits—this is one aspect of the synergy that I seek to define in describing the various aspects of our changing reading culture. Thus, to give a very particular instance, the sudden and wide adoption of "frames" in Internet sites can be seen as a way of taking the information in a site and exposing it structurally on a constant basis. As the reader works through the specific pages of information, there is always at hand this exposed structure, this navigational aid to the site, since the table of contents or indexing function is no longer an optional helpful feature for the reader but essential, on an ongoing basis, to the system of reading. That is, *the navigational aid has in some sense become primary.*

Much of what professors in the humanities seem to have to teach their students is how to read more slowly, more linearly, with more attention to the details of the text as it plays out, since these reading habits are increasingly uncommon and, for many tasks, sad as it may seem, rather irrelevant. A couple of years ago, a student, to my astonishment, told me that she found it easier to read, and easier to remember the things she read, on an Internet site than in a book. At the time, I was floored. It assaulted every idea I had of the advantages of print, of the metaphor I held to be dominant of the permanence of the printed book versus the transitoriness of the computer screen, of my internal picture of the frenetic, interrupted, distracted nature of computer reading, in which one is constantly tempted away from the text toward a new link, a new text. But I am belatedly coming to understand, I think, that a computer text, with its exposed structure and "sound bite"–sized bits of text, can facilitate comprehension and retention for someone growing up under the new paradigm of reading, where the navigational aids are primary, the informational digest secondary, and the text itself only tertiary. To a certain extent, that is, my student and I were talking past each other, since we meant something very different by "reading," being in, as it were, rather different reading cultures. It is this sort of thing I mean when I state that the "electronic revolution" seems in part informed by a basic change in the paradigm of reading.

What the New Reading Culture May Mean for Education

The educational consequences of the paradigm shift, if I am right in my own cultural reading, cannot be underestimated. A strong awareness of this shift in the way students process and retain text can help in effective learning. For example, in accommodating to the reading culture of the Web, I have found that my class notes (which I routinely post to the Web) become increasingly organized in a top-down fashion, increasingly structured, increasingly oriented toward the presentation of a radical synopsis of the material, even in the teaching of linear texts such as Homer or Vergil. Jay Bolter has argued, perhaps rightly, that the hypertextual environment encourages an aphoristic tendency, since each structural element in a written text becomes a linkable unit, thus potentially segregated from the linear sequence (Bolter 1991, p. ix). The tendency to aphorism, to expression in kernels of thought, need not be reductionist. In my own experiments with Web-based teaching of classical literature, I have found that use of on-line lecture notes has had the following consequences:

1. The weaker students find it easier to absorb and understand the material, since they no longer have to rely on their own muddled outlines and digests. The passivity may not in every way seem desirable, but I can report not only that many weaker students perform better but also that they pay more attention in class and seem much more involved in, and thoughtful about, these difficult ancient texts.

2. Since the "information" is available on the Web, I feel free both to include a great many more items, such as examples from the text, or links to other resources, than we could ever work through in class. Moreover, I have increasingly felt free to skip simpler sections altogether when class time seems better spent exploring one section in more detail.

3. Since the students are explicitly responsible for the Web materials, rather than what we may or may not cover in class, all the students are exposed to many more ideas than we can cover in class, and the stronger students work through the many examples—which is the only way to begin to get at the richness of texture of the literary text underlying my schematic analyses. The professorial narrative becomes, then, reduced and restructured on one hand but expanded and made more open-ended on the other. It no longer matches what goes on in the classroom. I can teach both at an elementary and an advanced level more or less simultaneously. Much more of the learning, suddenly, begins to take place outside of the classroom: the grappling with the Web-based professorial narrative seems to lead to a great deal more interaction among the students outside of class, as they work through these

materials, and the "class" becomes at times almost like a commentary on the "virtual class" in which we are all studying. That this sort of class can be so successful—a class where linear presentation is constantly interrupted or ignored altogether, where "kernelized" analysis is given precedence, even though we are studying literary texts, where there is constant diversion toward illustrative or related materials—begins, however, to make sense in the context of the new reading culture. It is not, in truth, the kind of class that I would prefer to take, but it *is* the kind of class that most of my students seem to prefer. The success of the class, in short, stems from the fact that I am attempting to work with, rather than fight against, the new habits of reading.

Sociocultural Aspects of Reading and Education

The physical and conceptual text is, however, only one part of the reading system, and arguably not the most important part. I want to turn back now to broaden the description of reading culture, for I have repeatedly broached, but never fully entered into, a discussion of one of the most fundamental aspects of the reading system, namely, the sociocultural construction of reading. As we shall see, I consider the sociocultural component not only crucial to reading culture generally but of special importance to the question of education. But first we need to gain a more vivid idea of this dimension of reading. As is my wont, I will start, this time quite briefly, with the ancient reading experience, again focusing on the reading of a prose literary text.

The ancient reader (by which I mean the educated person listening to the trained lector) is comfortably disposed: lying on a couch, relaxed, and often, perhaps usually, among friends. The attitude is not one of digesting information, or of a scholastic critical reaction, but either pure aesthetic pleasure or that sort of intellectual contention familiar to us in its extreme (and idealized) form from such sources as Plato and Athenaeus. The enjoyment of the lection is perhaps often interrupted by remarks or even debate: the text is a guide and springboard to conversation and discussion, constituting intellectual and aesthetic pleasure in a tightly bound, elite group. Note how social and textual event interlock. The physical text is beautiful, the reading is slow, the lector is well trained for the task of bringing the text alive to the hearers, the reading unfolds along with the book roll itself in a sequential and leisurely manner for a limited time, the comfortable setting bespeaks the wealth, culture, and refinement of those sharing in the experience, the difficulty of the text bespeaks their education. As a sociocultural *system* this reading experience begins to make sense, to take on flesh.

Now let us at a leap jump from antiquity back to our own time and compare and contrast this ancient scenario with a type of reading we all know well, namely, reading within the context of a humanities classroom. There are no couches, no continuous oral reading from the text, no luxuriousness (at least not at my university), but the scene is oddly similar in certain ways: the use of a text as a springboard to intellectual discourse; the tightly bound group that validates itself using a text that is important to a shared sense of culture; the comfortable feeling of the selectness of the group. But now let's turn this scene around and ask, pointedly: Why is it that students so commonly find difficult texts such as Homer's *Iliad* or Plato's *Republic* (or Dante or Baudelaire or Goethe) deeply exciting *within the context of a class?* If they do not read these texts in college, most of these same people, after all, as forty-something stockbrokers or business executives, are not likely to find these texts very engaging. Why do young men and women who find Greek or Sanskrit or Swahili captivating as students rarely read these languages once they graduate? What specifically is the nature of the magical web that a good teacher is able to spin?

A great deal, I think, depends on the sociocultural construction of the reading group, and much of what we do in higher education, both institutionally and individually, is to work toward the construction of particular types of reading groups. In a successful humanities class, we are not so much teaching texts as creating a reading society, which finds self-validation in the negotiated construction on meaning from these texts. That is, institutionally we work, for instance, toward creating the disposition that knowledge of and directed engagement with particular humanities texts is socioculturally important: it is part of what you *need* to know to be "educated," to become part of the cultured elite of society. Individually, we as teachers work toward creating the disposition that a particular text (the one we are studying in the class) is meaningful and relevant: it is part of what you need to apprehend the knowledge and to experience that sense of meaningfulness that bonds the group together as a productive, self-validating unit. These group dynamics— the construction of the attitude in the reader that Plato is *important,* that Plato *should be interesting*—are fundamental to education and fundamental to the high intellectual experience. Reading is the individual's construction of meaning, but it is never wholly interior; rather, sociocultural influences always inform the meaning that the reader seeks to construct, as anthropologists and linguists increasingly recognize (compare, for example, Heath 1983; Street 1984; and Finnegan 1988).

It is here that I find the new techno-culture so deeply exciting for education. Techno-culture seems to me a rich opportunity if looked on in light of the construction of reading communities. Although central to what we do as educators, construction of communities is tough in the context of much humanistic education, whether the less common languages and literatures (today comprising once-popular languages such as French, German, and Russian) or the many other subjects increasingly perceived as "impractical" (including philosophy, world religion, or art history) and thus often wanting for students beyond the introductory level. What I have in mind goes, however, beyond courses that use the Internet to link up solitary or small groups of students into a virtual class. The sense of a techno-culture that underlies many contemporary reading communities, from chat rooms to discussion groups to loose networks of e-mail correspondents, is potentially a powerful tool that can extend beyond the construction of typical class activity and a tool that can be used to access groups beyond the eighteen-to-twenty-two set that American education typically targets. American arts councils, whether they promote opera, symphony, art, or theater, have long been successful at creating a *life-long sense of engagement* from targeted persons. Interestingly, many of these people do not in fact have a profound passion for art or music or theater; rather, they share an interest that seems to them culturally important. For our purposes, what is interesting is the participation of the arts council itself in the negotiation and construction of the cultural group, in promoting and indeed exploiting that important sense of a culturally self-validating society.

Imagine an America in which it becomes part of the social scene of the educated not simply to go to the occasional opera or play but to do cool intellectual things over the Internet, an America in which a normal cultural aspiration for any educated person—the cool (that is, socially validating) thing to do—is to get together with your intellectual group and discuss language, literature, and culture. Imagine a set of educators who conspire, as it were, to use the Internet to link and organize persons with specific shared interests, to facilitate and promote directed techno-cultural communities, who spread many seeds in the hope that various small techno-cultural communities will take root. Imagine intellectual groups, be they speakers of Ukrainian, students of antiquity, or alumni of Oberlin, who use the techno-cultural community to get that sense of an ongoing, broadly shared mission, even as they are also able to identify local people with whom they could share more conventional social intercourse.

I am a classicist: I am no seer, I bear no words from Apollo, and this scenario may well seem fantastic. But let us turn, one final time, to the ancient Mediterranean. In a provincial watering hole deep in the Egyptian desert, at a town named Oxyrhynchus, a group of ancient Greeks, in the midst of an Egyptian culture for generations, used the reading of Homer, Euripides, Sappho, and Aristotle as a means of maintaining their sense of cultural identity, of keeping their Greekness—but also as a means of maintaining their sense of education and civilization even while the desert encroached on all sides. Two millennia later in Britain, in the early days of the twentieth century, the Egypt Exploration Fund, a nonacademic, professionally diverse club of the intellectually curious, would meet frequently, and with great excitement, to study these same texts as they were being dug from the sands of Oxyrhynchus—in part an expression of their sense of belonging to the educated class of a great imperial power.

If sociocultural groups could find life-long intellectual community in provincial Greco-Roman Egypt and in Edwardian England, why not in technologically sophisticated America? The sense of belonging to an educated, cultured group can be a powerful force and is one that we, as educators, labor to construct but one that we let pass out of our hands the moment our charges leave the university. We may be able to make better progress both in our ability to connect with undergraduates and in the goal of life-long humanistic learning if we start to think of the use of technology not simply as a classroom or research tool but as a part of how contemporary people negotiate the construction of reading communities and if we try to think through specifically how to use to advantage the cachet and "sex appeal" of the technoculture to facilitate the construction of broadly based, continuing, specialized communities of readers.

In this brief essay, I have taken time to look at only a couple of aspects of our contemporary reading culture, a culture that seems, if I am right, to be shifting in an important way. Obviously, to do a proper job I would need to look at the reading system from a greater variety of viewpoints, to try to see what other elements I can isolate that differ from the reading-from-a-printed book paradigm. These would include the use of graphic symbolism, the influence of video and audio technologies, the aesthetics of electronic tools and how aesthetics influence sociocultural constructions, the intersection of virtual and interpersonal communications in the reading society, and so forth. But I hope that even this very prolegomenal treatment of our contemporary reading culture suffices to suggest some ways in which thinking through reading *as a system* may be able to help as we try to sort out the paradigm shift going on about us.

This written record developed from two oral papers delivered in the fall of 1998, one at Oberlin College (a celebration of the career of Professor Nathan A. Greenberg), the other at the Massachusetts Institute of Technology (a conference titled "Transformations: Technology, Foreign Languages, and Undergraduate Education"). The sections on ancient reading culture rely on, and in some cases summarize or paraphrase, the more detailed presentation of evidence and analysis in Johnson (2000). The comments on teaching with Web-based materials reflect in particular my experience in a series of classical civilization courses taught at Bucknell University from 1997 to 1999.

References

Bolter, J. D. (1991). *Writing Space: The Computer, Hypertext, and the History of Writing.* Hillsdale, N.J.: Lawrence Erlbaum Associates.

Carruthers, M. J. (1990). *The Book of Memory: A Study of Memory in Medieval Culture.* Cambridge: Cambridge University Press.

Cribiore, R. (1996). *Writing, Teachers, and Students in Graeco-Roman Egypt.* Atlanta, Ga.: Scholars.

Eisenstein, E. (1979). *The Printing Press as an Agent of Change.* Cambridge: Cambridge University Press.

Finnegan, R. (1988). *Literacy and Orality: Studies in the Technology of Communication.* Oxford: Blackwell.

Goody, J. (1977). *The Domestication of the Savage Mind.* Cambridge: Cambridge University Press.

Goody, J., and I. Watt. (1963). The Consequences of Literacy. *Contemporary Studies in Society and History* 5: 304–45. Republished in *Literacy in Traditional Societies,* edited by J. Goody (Cambridge: Cambridge University Press, 1968), 27–68.

Havelock, E. (1963). *Preface to Plato.* Cambridge: Cambridge University Press.

Heath, S. B. (1983). *Ways with Words.* Cambridge: Cambridge University Press.

Johnson, W. A. (2000). Towards a Sociology of Reading in Classical Antiquity. *American Journal of Philology* 121: 593–627.

———. (2003). *Bookrolls and Scribes in Oxyrhynchus.* Toronto: University of Toronto Press.

McLuhan, M. (1962). *The Gutenberg Galaxy: The Making of Typographic Man.* Toronto: University of Toronto Press.

Miller, K. (1998). Tough Luck for Editors, *Times Literary Supplement* 4970 (July 3), 7.

Olson, D. (1994). *The World on Paper: The Conceptual and Cognitive Implications of Reading and Writing.* Cambridge: Cambridge University Press.

Saenger, P. (1997). *Space Between Words: The Origins of Silent Reading.* Stanford: Stanford University Press.

Street, B. V. (1984). *Literacy in Theory and Practice.* Cambridge: Cambridge University Press.

Thomas, R. (1992). *Orality and Literacy in Ancient Greece.* Cambridge: Cambridge University Press.

Turner, E. G. (1987). *Greek Manuscripts of the Ancient World.* 2d ed., revised by P. J. Parsons. London: Institute for Classical Studies, University College London.

Wingo, E. O. (1972). *Latin Punctuation in the Classical Age.* The Hague: Mouton.

2

Literacy and Cognition

MARK TURNER

Fifty thousand years ago, more or less, during the Upper Paleolithic Age, our ancestors began the most spectacular advance in human history. Before then, we were a negligible group of large mammals. Afterward, we were supreme.

The archaeological record suggests that during the Upper Paleolithic our ancestors acquired a cognitively modern human imagination, furnishing them with the ability to invent new concepts and to assemble new and dynamic mental patterns. As a result, human beings developed art, science, religion, culture, refined tool use, and language. What happened? How can we human beings do what we do?

Before this period, the knowledge an animal could have and the range of behavior it could enact were, relative to the standards of modern human beings, sharply limited. But in the Upper Paleolithic, one species became astonishingly different. Our ancestors became "cognitively modern," that is, able to learn and to know many different things that are not shared throughout the species. It became possible for some members of this species to develop and deploy complex conceptual structures that were unavailable to other members of the species. Literacy became an issue, if by "literacy" we mean a learned ability to deploy elaborate conceptual structures (such as a particular language, or writing, or the concept of a particular set of rituals) that some other members of the species lack and that they cannot come to possess and deploy unless they undertake a protracted process of learning. Before the Upper Paleolithic, there were basically no phenomena of literacy. Afterward, literacy became crucial to human existence.

This is our condition now. Some of us write English and use dollars, others write Spanish and use pesos. Some of us read, and some of us do not. Some of us know very precisely how to behave during Easter in Moscow, others know how to behave during Easter in Paris, and others know how to behave during a seder in Los Angeles.

Gilles Fauconnier and I, working in collaboration, have proposed that what happened during the Upper Paleolithic was this: an apparently small group of human beings finally reached an evolutionary stage in which they attained a more powerful level of a cognitive ability possessed to some degree by all mammals. This cognitive ability is "conceptual integration," and the advanced version of conceptual integration that makes literacy possible is "double-scope integration."

The ability to do conceptual integration at the double-scope level made it possible for us to develop many individual conceptual products that look superficially quite different, such as grammar and mathematics, art and religion, ritual and humor, watches and money, marriage and science. "Literacy" is a measure of how some human beings differ from others in the conceptual structures they can deploy. Those differences are the result of our capacity for double-scope integration. Other species do not have this capacity and so do not have literacy or illiteracy.

The cognitive operation of conceptual integration, also called "blending," is very complex. It has a set of overarching goals, a set of constitutive principles, and a set of guiding principles. There is a taxonomy of types of conceptual integration networks. Most important, the cognitive operation of conceptual integration does not work in the way we might have imagined.

In this chapter I cannot possibly introduce the principles of conceptual integration at any depth. I shall instead illustrate conceptual integration with a few examples, referring the reader for details to Turner (1996), Fauconnier and Turner (1998), Turner and Fauconnier (1999), and especially the blending Web site (Turner 1999–), which presents research on the subject by many researchers in many fields. Then I shall discuss the importance of advanced forms of conceptual integration for learning a language and for learning prose styles.

It is easy to give immediately obvious examples of conceptual blending. Such examples are all around us, and the conceptual integration networks on which they rely play a major role in our mental existence. But these examples are profoundly misleading, since they give the impression that we recognize blending as it happens. On the contrary, almost all blending happens below the horizon of observation. These obvious examples are also misleading in other ways, since any one of them has special features, inviting us to make the error of thinking that those special features are essential to the operation of conceptual blending.

Consider, as one of these misleadingly pyrotechnic examples, a little cartoon in which snails are playing hide-and-seek ("Pretzel Logic" by Frank Deale). The seeker snail, covering his eyes and leaning against a rock, is counting "1000, 999, 998, 997, 996, 995, 994, 993, 992, . . ." while all the other snails are headed off to find hiding places. In one input mental space, there are snails, which move slowly. In another input mental space, there are human children playing hide and seek. As always in conceptual integration, we construct at least a partial mapping between these inputs. In this case, the individual snails correspond to the individual human children.

These two mental arrays are fundamentally opposed in nearly every way one would want to explore, and they certainly do not share an organizing conceptual frame. Snails do not play elaborate social games, or count numbers, frontwards or backwards, for example. In the blend, there is new meaning, emergent structure: snails can play hide-and-seek, have language and numbers, can count out loud, and so on. They count ordinal numbers in a way that is alien for the seeker child in hide-and-seek, who (at least as I know the game) does not count backwards from one thousand. The act of counting backward from one thousand during hide-and-seek originates in complex ways from conceptual integration. When we read the cartoon, we notice immediately that the snail counts backward from a thousand and know immediately that this takes a very long time and infer that this pattern of counting is necessary because the snails who are trying to hide need a lot of time in which to do so. We probably do not notice that the reason the snail counts backward is that a cartoon speech bubble with "1, 2, 3, 4, 5, 6, 7, 8, 9, . . ." would not communicate to us that the snail is in the process of counting all the way to one thousand. So the cartoonist, who wants us to construct the right snails-playing-hide-and-seek blend, in which the snails are going to take nearly forever to hide, makes the seeker snail count backward from one thousand, so we will infer unambiguously that the count is long.

Snail hide-and-seek is a "double-scope" integration network. In such a network, the inputs have different (and often clashing) organizing conceptual frames (snails in a garden versus children playing hide-and-seek), and the blend has an organizing frame that includes part of each of those frames and also has emergent structure of its own. In a double-scope integration network, the organizing frames of both inputs make important contributions to the blend, and their sharp differences offer the possibility of rich clashes. Far from blocking the construction of an integration network, such clashes offer challenges to the imagination, and the resulting blends can turn out to be highly creative.

Once we recognize a particular conceptual integration network, we often come to see that it is merely one instance among many of a slightly abstract mental template that is deployed repeatedly throughout the culture. In fact, knowing such templates is the major component of cultural literacy. For example, the particular snail-hide-and-seek blend that we construct to make sense of the cartoon is merely one instance among many of a conceptual integration template in which one conceptual input has a nonhuman species or object, the other has a human activity, and the blend has the blended object engaged in something close to the human activity, but the blended activity is modified in some crucial and often humorous way because the object is unlike the human being in some crucial way. For example, another cartoon shows an octopus parent playing "Which Hand?" with its offspring ("Speed Bump" by Dave Coverly). The octopus parent has all eight of its tentacles behind its back and is holding a treat in one of them. It says to its offspring, "I've got a treat for you . . . Guess which tentacle!" The glum offspring is thinking, "I hate this game!" In another "Speed Bump" cartoon, one twelve-inch ruler says to another, in a comment on two other rulers who are walking hand in hand, "Looks like true love . . . In fact, I hear he converted to metric for her." And in another, called "Worm Moms," the mother worm says to her little worms, who are with her inside some underground worm tunnel, "It's pouring rain outside, and you two are in here watching TV? Out! Out!" Gary Larson is of course the recognized master of this genre of cartoon.

These funny little blends are immediately intelligible and seem almost trivial. In fact, they are exceptionally complex double-scope integrations that develop considerable emergent structure and require powerful inferencing. We do not reject them as insane even though they blend two things that conflict very strongly.

Grammatical Constructions

Although these little cartoons can seem unimportant, language is surely all-important for the study of literacy, and just as surely very difficult to analyze. The central problem of language is that a system of relatively few forms must be able to prompt for the construction of vast ranges of meaning.

How have human beings solved this problem? The answer is, by sophisticated conceptual integration. Expressions do not encode meanings but instead prompt us to use our mental power to do conceptual integration to construct meaning. The scope and range of conceptual integration is vast, and so a few grammatical forms can be used to prompt for vast ranges of meaning construction. Literacy, or at least one fundamental type of literacy, consists of knowing how the particular grammatical constructions of a language prompt for particular conceptual integration networks. This knowledge must be learned. What human beings do not have to learn is the ability for conceptual integration itself. That ability is part of human nature.

Consider, as an illustration, the English resultative construction. I will consider here how knowing this grammatical construction depends on knowing a conceptual integration network and how to use it. My analysis is meant to stand for a general analysis of the way in which learning a language is learning systems of prompts for conceptual integration networks.

Suppose that there is a room, and that its walls and ceiling are not pristine white, and that Kathy acquires and gathers appropriate painting materials, prepares the room, and performs many actions of rolling or brushing white paint with instruments until the white paint covers major surfaces in the room, that the paint dries, and that thereafter the walls and ceiling of the room are pristine white. These unintegrated events are given a high degree of integration when expressed as "Kathy painted the room white." We know this sentence does not mean that she painted it because it was white, or painted it because she is white, or painted it with primer so that the painters would later be able to paint it white, but rather that she painted it with the result that it became white. Even though there are no individual words in the expression that explicitly indicate that *white* is a result, the grammatical form itself assigns white to the role *result* and the room to the role *patient*.

This grammatical construction, the English resultative, analyzed by Goldberg (1995), has a conceptual half and a formal half. Its conceptual half is the blending of two conceptual inputs. The first input is an integrated conceptual schema, R, which structures prototypical cases such as *paint* and *dye*. R includes an agent role a (for example, Kathy); a role e (for example, painted) that subsumes causal action, means, manner of the action, and caused event leading to a result for a patient; a role x (for example, the room) that subsumes both the patient of the action and an entity for which there is a result r; and a result role r (for example, white). Formally, in English, R is associated with the form NP1 V NP2 ADJ, as follows: a with NP1, e with V, x with NP2, and r with ADJ. "Mike pressed the wallpaper flat."

Input 2 is an unintegrated causal sequence. In this sequence, there is an agent a' who acts; this act is causal for a second conceptual bundle, containing an entity x' for which there is a result r', and some event e' whose result is r'.

In the cross-space mapping between input R and input 2, unproblematically, a corresponds to a', x corresponds to x', and r corresponds to r'. Also, e in R corresponds to some not uniquely specified e' in input 2. The blend has roles a'', e'', x'', and r'', mapped from R. Content for those roles is provided by input 2. The blend inherits syntax from R, so that a'' is assigned to NP1, x'' is assigned to NP2, and r'' is assigned to ADJ. But for e'', there is more than one possibility, because there is more than one way to map e.

If e in input R corresponds to the agent's action in input 2, the blend inherits that action, and a verb expressing it will show up in the V position of the syntactic form NP V NP ADJ, as in "She kissed him unconscious" or "She rubbed it raw." *Kiss* and *rub* are not prototypical instances of R, but the construction evokes a blending with R as an input, and so both of these expressions evoke resultative meanings.

If e is mapped to the causal link, an appropriate causal verb appears, as in "She made the floor dirty" or "She got him angry."

If e is mapped onto the event resulting in r', a verb expressing that event will show up in the V position, as in "She ran them ragged" (where she herself did not run), "She burned it black," "She bent it straight," "She bled him dry," and "She boiled the pan dry" (note that she did not boil and that she did not boil the pan).

Conceptual blending allows other elements from input 2 to map onto e'' and to be reflected by a single verb form:

> "She hammered it flat." *Hammer* expresses action but points to the instrument associated with that action.
> "She set it free," "She set the flame low." *Set* expresses causality and points to something about the aspect of the event.
> "She dimmed the background grey." *Dim* expresses not only the result but also something about the manner of the event the result of which is that the background is dim, as with "She cleared the screen blank."
> "She worked it loose." *Work* expresses something about the aspect of the action.

The blend of input R and input 2 yields emergent structure at the grammatical level, in the form of new roles added to verbs. Consider Goldberg's example, in which John's talking loudly causes him to become hoarse. We cannot use the verbs available for the unintegrated input 2 to say *"He talked himself," meaning that he was the patient of his talking. But the roles in the blend are mapped from input R, so the blend does have a role for *patient, x"*, and, in the syntax inherited from R, *patient* is assigned to NP2. In the blend, *talk* does have a patient role and a result role, added to it by the construction. So we can say, "He talked himself hoarse."

The English resultative construction depends on conceptual integration in an even more fundamental way: input R is itself already a conventional blend. I shall call its two input spaces input R1 and input R2. Input R1 has an agent whose act causes an object to move along a path from one location to another. Input R2 has an agent whose act causes an event with a result for a patient. In the blend R, the patient is an object and the result is its new location. R is an abstract, entrenched, and conventional metaphoric blend. In R, changing state is moving along a path from one location to another. As Goldberg observes, this path is single and in a single landscape. Goldberg explores the unexpected consequences of the fact that R has this emergent structure. Specifically, although a causal action can have multiple results, the singleness of the path prevents us from getting two co-occurring resultatives of one action, as in the ungrammatical sentence *"She kicked him black-and-blue dead," on the reading that *black-and-blue* and *dead* both result from *kicked* (and *black-and-blue* is not a determiner for *dead*). Also, the path's restriction to a single landscape requires that resultatives do not combine with directional phrases that would yield both a path in a spatial landscape and a path in a metaphoric landscape of states, as in the ungrammatical sentences *"Sam kicked Bill black and blue out of the room" and *"Sam kicked Bill out of the room black and blue," both on the reading that *black and blue* is the result of *kicked*. But since prepositional complements that are not directionals do not result in paths in two landscapes, they can combine with resultatives, as in the grammatical sentence "He loaded the wagon full with hay."

We see, then, that the English resultative construction prompts for conceptual blending that has as one input R, but R itself is the blend of R1 and R2. Multiple stages of conceptual blending are in fact extremely common in the kinds of knowledge that count as instances of human literacy.

Consider now the English ditransitive construction, also analyzed by Goldberg (1995), which prompts for double-scope conceptual integration with remarkable ferocity. A prototypical example of the ditransitive is "Bill gave Mary a gift." The verb *gave* by itself evokes a conceptual schema in which a causal agent, by some means, successfully causes the transfer of an object to a recipient. I will call this schema D. The verb *pour* does not by itself evoke D ("The water poured out of the drain pipe"), yet when *pour* is used in the ditransitive syntax ("Bill poured Mary some wine"), the construction itself evokes schema D.

The use of the English ditransitive prompts us to integrate, conceptually, some unintegrated events with the highly integrated ditransitive schema D, to create a blend O. But the organizing schema of O is *double-scope*, that is, it takes organizing schema–level structure from *both* inputs. Although Goldberg does not use the model of conceptual integration, I think various double-scope blends are implicit in her analysis, as follows. If D and the organizing schema for the unintegrated events match closely, their blend takes its organizing schema from both of them. This is the case for verbs that inherently signify acts of giving an object (*give, pass, hand, serve, feed*), verbs of instantaneous causation of ballistic motion (*throw, toss, slap, kick, poke, fling, shoot*), and verbs of continuous causation in a deictically specified direction (*bring, take*). But if the verb is a verb of refusal (*refuse, deny*) as in "The boss denied Bill a raise," then the blend O takes the potential recipient and the potential patient from D but takes the causing of the not receiving from input 2, with the result that D is counterfactual with respect to O. If the verb is a verb of giving with associated satisfaction conditions (*guarantee, promise, owe*), then the blend takes from input 2 kinds of causal structure for reception that are not in D. If the verb involves a scene of creation (*bake, make, build, cook, sew, knit*) or a verb of obtaining (*get, grab, win, earn*), then O takes from D intention to cause the recipient to receive the patient, but not necessarily success. If the verb is a verb of permission (*permit, allow*), then O takes enablement from input 2 rather than successful causation from D. If the verb is a verb of future transfer (*leave, bequeath, allocate, reserve, grant*), then the blend takes future transfer from input 2 rather than successful causation of present reception from D. These blends fall into conceptual classes, each class with its own two-sided organizing schema and each with its associated classes of verbs. These double-scope blends, and the use of the ditransitive to evoke them, can become conventional, so that the ditransitive can, as a matter of convention, be associated not only with the prototypical schema D but also with these various abstract double-scope blends.

In fact, this survey only scratches the surface of the conventional blends that have D as one input. Again, although Goldberg does not use the model of conceptual blending, there is a taxonomy of metaphoric blends implicit in her analysis, as follows: (1) D is conventionally blended with an abstract schema for *causing an effect for an entity;* this produces a metaphoric blend in which the effect is an object and causing the effect for the entity is causing the object to come to the entity. This conventional blend inherits the ditransitive syntax from D, so that one can say, "The medicine brought him relief" and "She gave me a headache." (2) D is conventionally blended with a schema for *communication;* this produces a metaphoric blend, analyzed by Reddy (1979), in which meaning is an object and communicating it to someone is giving it to a recipient. This conventional blend inherits the ditransitive syntax from D, so that one can say, "She told Jo a fairy tale." (3) There is a conventional blend of *motion of an object toward a recipient* with *perceiving*. In the blend, perception is reception of the "perception" by the recipient. This metaphoric blend is exploited as a basis for producing a more detailed metaphoric blend, with D as one input and *causing someone to perceive* as the other. In this more detailed blend, perception is an object and causing someone to perceive it is transferring it to him. This inherits the ditransitive syntax from D, so that one can say, "He showed Bob the view." (4) D is conventionally blended with *directing an action at another person.* In this metaphoric blend, the action is an object and directing it at another person is transferring it to her as recipient. This inherits the ditransitive syntax from D, so that one can say, "She threw him a parting glance." (5) There is a conventional metaphoric blend of *constructing an object out of parts* and *developing an argument.* In this blend, facts and assumptions used in arguing are parts used in constructing. This is exploited as a basis for a more detailed blend, of D and *granting facts and assumptions to an arguer.* In this more detailed blend, granting a fact or assumption to the arguer is transferring it to her as recipient. This inherits the ditransitive syntax from D, and so one can say, "I'll give you that assumption."

There is an interesting final case. Goldberg observes correctly that in expressions such as "Slay me a dragon," one of the input schemata has an agent performing an action for the benefit of someone else, and the first postverbal noun refers to the beneficiary while the second postverbal noun refers not to what the recipient receives but rather to what the causal agent acts on. I offer the following explanation, which I think follows the spirit of Goldberg's analysis closely even though it uses the model of conceptual blending and a slightly different array of input schemas. D inheres in a more detailed but highly conventional schema D′. In D′, someone brings a benefit to someone by transferring an object to him. "Bill gave me a dollar" is typically understood as meaning not only that a dollar was transferred but that a benefit (for example, the ability to purchase) was conferred by means of the transfer. "Mary poured Bob a glass of wine" is typically understood as meaning not only that a glass of wine was poured with the intention of transfer but also that a benefit (for example, wherewithal for pleasure or nourishment) was intended to be conferred by means of pouring and (intended) giving. Of course, D is not always an instance of D′: "My child handed me his banana peel" is probably D but not D′. Nonetheless, the ditransitive syntax is attached not only to D but also to D′, and, depending on vocabulary and context, it is usually a good strategy to try to interpret ditransitive syntax as evoking D'. In the ditransitive construction, the second postverbal noun always refers to the patient (metaphoric or not) of the causal agent's action, whether or not that patient is also the transferred object (metaphoric or not). What happens in "Slay me a dragon" or "Sing me a song" is a double-scope, selective projection to the blend, with D' as one input. We project from D' to the blend a causal agent performing an action on an object (metaphoric or not) and the intended consequent conferral of a benefit on someone, but we do not project from D' the reception of an object. The blend inherits the ditransitive syntax associated with D', and, as always in the ditransitive, the patient of the causal action is assigned to the second post-verbal noun.

Using their basic human ability for double-scope blending, the speakers in different language communities develop different grammatical construc-tions. Even when these constructions seem to be related, there are typically crucial differences between them. The French resultative construction has a different grammatical form ("Catherine a peint le mur *en* blanc"). The En-glish caused motion construction ("He kicked the ball over the fence," "He floated the boat across the pond," "We teased him out of his mind") is much more promiscuous (linguists say "productive") than its French cousin: the English construction can be used to express kinds of causal action and caused motion that are not accepted by the French version. In English, when we want to express caused action, we say something like "I made Paul run," but the French would say, "J'ai fait courir Paul." Hebrew, as Nili Mandelblit (1995) shows, has a different set of constructions to convey such a meaning. Hebrew verbs all consist of a skeleton of consonants (the "root"), slotted into some vowel pattern or prefix + vowel pattern. Such a vowel or prefix + vowel pattern is called a *binyan*. The consonants carry the "core meaning" of the verb. There are seven major *binyanim* in Hebrew (the capital C's stand for the root consonants to be inserted): *CaCaC, CuCaC, CiCeC, niCCaC, hiCCiC, huCCaC,* and *hitCaCeC*. Mandelblit shows that each binyan prompts for a particular blending schema. Consider, for example, the binyan *hiCCiC* (termed *hif'il*), and the root verb *r-u-c*, meaning "run." These two con-structions are blended at both the conceptual and the formal levels to give a resultant construction, a verb, *hiruic*, written (or rather transliterated) *heric*, that means "make to run." In this way, Hebrew can express "I made Paul run" using a single main verb, because its grammatical constructions differ from those available for this purpose in English. Learning a language is learning these blending templates. Moreover, as Israel (1996) shows, grammatical con-structions develop diachronically through changes in the blending patterns they evoke.

Reading, Writing, and Style

Reading and writing—"literacy" in the everyday sense—of course depend absolutely on the existence of grammatical constructions, which have been produced through blending, but they also depend on blending in another crucial way. In reading and writing, we see physical marks on stone or paper or a computer screen, and these marks are circulated through the community. By themselves, these marks are meaningless. But someone who is literate in the everyday sense has a general blending template for writing and reading. In it, one input has someone talking and the other input has some medium with marks, and in the blend, the marks and the speech are fused in impressive ways. The projection to the blend from the inputs is creative and imaginative. The blending template does not say what is being said in the blend. For that, we need a material anchor: a particular letter, book, or inscription. The emergent integrated activities of writing and reading are strikingly different from speech in nearly all aspects. But the blend and the speech input are connected, and we know therefore how to interpret the blend. When we look at writing, or when we write, we are dealing cognitively not only with distinguishing between physical marks but instead with a conceptual blend in which these marks are integrated with speech.

Because we know different human-scale scenes in which someone is speaking, there are different prose styles. Thomas and Turner (1994; see classicprose.com) analyze prose style from this theoretical perspective. Here, I will present briefly, as an illustration, one particular prose style, classic style. Here is an example:

> Mme. de Chevreuse avait beaucoup d'esprit, d'ambition et de beauté; elle était galante, vive, hardie, entreprenante; elle se servait de tous ses charmes pour réussir dans ses desseins, et elle a presque toujours porté malheur aux personnes qu'elle y a engagées. (La Rochefoucauld, *Mémoires* [See Thomas and Turner 1994, p. 16])

> (Madame de Chevreuse had sparkling intelligence, ambition, and beauty in plenty; she was flirtatious, lively, bold, enterprising; she used all her charms to push her projects to success, and she almost always brought disaster to those she encountered on her way.)

In classic style, the input with someone talking has a particular and rich structure. In it, one person is talking to another and the occasion is informal. The speaker's motive is that he has recognized some truth worth presenting, and his entire purpose is to present that recognition to the listener, to make it possible for the listener to see what the speaker has seen. The speaker and the listener are both competent. They are symmetrical in having a classic intellect; indeed, the listener could take the next turn in the conversation and perform similarly. The speaker thinks before speaking, and what he says, although it is talk, is perfect, and naturally so, since it is the product of a classic mind in full command of a language. Language, in this conception, is adequate to present anything. The truth the speaker has recognized is not in any way radically contingent on point of view or idiosyncrasy—it may be that the listener does not know Hebrew or never lived during the seventeenth century, but these are merely accidental impediments to recognition; the listener has no fundamental incapacity to recognize what the writer recognizes. The speech is a perfect window on its subject: it shows what it has to show. The speaker does not acknowledge that his style or language might itself be the subject of attention. The occasion is not rushed, although the speech has the efficiency that comes of having a classic mind. Neither speaker nor listener is pressured by deadlines or a job to do, such as making investments, fixing a machine, or completing a school assignment. That is, the presentation is not subordinate to some other purpose. The speaker has no need to persuade the listener that he should listen, and in fact no ambition to persuade the listener: all the speaker has to do is present the recognition properly, and the listener will see.

This input is the model for the style. It is the one that is assumed by the style. In fact, there do exist a few occasions that actually come close to fitting this assumed scene. One is being in the field with a human guide, who points things out. Consequently, field guides and guidebooks are a natural genre for the use of classic style. Here is an example:

Northern Shrike (*Lanius excubitor*)

Unusual among songbirds, shrikes prey on small birds and rodents, catching them with the bill and sometimes impaling them on thorns or barbed wire for storage. Like other northern birds that depend on rodent populations, the Northern Shrike's movements are cyclical, becoming more abundant in the South when northern rodent populations are low. At times they hunt from an open perch, where they sit motionless until prey appears; at other times they hover in the air ready to pounce on anything that moves. (John Bull and John Farrand Jr., *The Audubon Society Field Guide to North American Birds, Eastern Region* [see Thomas and Turner 1994, p. 115])

But prose styles are generally useful, because we can blend that assumed scene with other, conflicting scenes. Suppose, for example, that the real situation is a job-seeking letter: the roles of interviewer and candidate are profoundly asymmetrical, the motive is greed, the purpose is to persuade the employer to offer the job, and so on. This real situation can be blended with the assumed scene to give a style in which the candidate in fact wants nothing from the interviewer, is entirely confident, and enjoys symmetry with the interviewer. The applicant is simply presenting truth. The result can be a very compelling letter. It is crucial to the power and utility of a prose style that its existing blending template for integrating marks in a medium with a model scene of speech can be further blended with a quite conflicting actual scene to produce a multiple-scope blend that in crucial ways includes some of the structure of the model scene.

What defines a general style is its conceptual blending template, not surface features. It is not possible to teach literacy in a prose style by teaching surface features. For example, students who try to understand classic style as a bundle of surface features cannot begin to locate the common stylistic basis of the following classic examples:

> The self cannot be escaped, but it can be, with ingenuity and hard work, distracted. (Donald Barthelme, "Daumier" [Thomas and Turner 1994, p. 163])

> Malgré son état liquide, le lait doit toujours être considéré comme un aliment et non comme une boisson . . . (*Nouveau Larousse Gastronomique* [Thomas and Turner 1994, p. 39])
> (In spite of its liquid state, milk must always be considered as a food and not as a beverage.)

> Although a dirty campaign was widely predicted, for the most part the politicians contented themselves with insults and lies. (Julian Barnes on the 1992 British parliamentary elections [Thomas and Turner 1994, p. 87])

> Hemorrhoids are actually varicose veins in the rectum. (First sentence of an anonymous brochure in a medical clinic, 1992 [Thomas and Turner 1994, p. 122])

> A portrait now in the possession of the descendants of the Kiryu clan shows Terukatsu sitting cross-legged on a tiger skin, fully clad in armor with a European breastplate, black-braided shoulder plates, taces and fur boots. His helmet is surmounted by enormous, sweeping horns, like a water buffalo's. He holds a tasseled baton of command in his right hand; his left hand is spread so wide on his thigh that the thumb reaches the scabbard of his sword. If he were not wearing armor, one could get some idea of his physique; dressed as he is, only the face is visible. It is not uncommon to see likenesses of heroes from the Period of Civil Wars clad in full armor, and Terukatsu's is very similar to those of Honda Heihachiro and Sakakibara Yasumasa that so often appear in history books. They all give an impression of great dignity and severity, but at the same time there is an uncomfortable stiffness and formality in the way they square their shoulders. (Junichiro Tanizaki, *The*

Secret History of the Lord of Musashi, translated by Anthony H. Chambers [Thomas and Turner 1994, p. 129])

Palabra por palabra, la versión de Galland es la peor escrita de todas, la más embustera y más débil, pero fue la mejor leída. Quienes intimaron con ella, conocieron la felicidad y el asombro. Su orientalismo, que ahora nos parece frugal, encandiló a cuantos aspiraban rapé y complotaban una tragedia en cinco actos. Doce primorosos volúmenes aparecieron de 1707 a 1717, doce volúmenes innumerablemente leídos y que pasaron a diversos idiomas, incluso el hindustani y el árabe. Nosotros, meros lectores anacrónicos del siglo veinte, percibimos en ellos el sabor dulzarrón del siglo dieciocho y no el desvanecido aroma oriental, que hace doscientos años determinó su innovación y su gloria. Nadie tiene la culpa del desencuentro y menos que nadie, Galland. (Jorge Luis Borges, "Los traductores de las 1001 noches" [Thomas and Turner 1994, p. 145])

(Word for word, Galland's version is the worst written, the most fraudulent and the weakest, but it was the most widely read. Readers who grew intimate with it experienced happiness and amazement. Its orientalism, which we now find tame, dazzled the sort of person who inhaled snuff and plotted tragedies in five acts. Twelve exquisite volumes appeared from 1707 to 1717, twelve volumes innumerably read, which passed into many languages, including Hindustani and Arabic. We, mere anachronistic readers of the twentieth century, perceive in these volumes the cloyingly sweet taste of the eighteenth century and not the evanescent oriental aroma that two hundred years ago was their innovation and their glory. No one is to blame for this missed encounter, least of all Galland.)

But once a student is introduced to the general blending template that defines classic style, the student can typically begin to work with some facility in that style in a matter of weeks.

A cultural blending template, once learned, operates with great complexity but almost entirely unconsciously. When the cognitively modern child, equipped with its human ability for blending, comes into the world, it undergoes an extremely active period of mastering the blending templates the culture has to offer—grammatical constructions, rituals, forms of representation, arithmetic, dance, and material anchors such as money and watches. It uses basic cognitive abilities to make sense of the cultural world in which it is immersed and learns these blending templates even though no one in its environment, least of all the child, can articulate with any sophistication what they are. After about age three or four, it spends a lifetime taking these blends apart and putting them back together in useful and creative ways. Immersed in a culture, it picks up the available styles, including the prose styles.

This picture of how we learn presents a great challenge to the teacher of foreign languages and cultures, not to say to the student. To learn a foreign language, and actually to learn its cultural styles, is to learn to deploy its conceptual blending schemes—for grammatical constructions, for reading, for writing, and for styles of writing. People who actually command these blending templates have no need to articulate them consciously or explicitly, and for the most part cannot. The child immersed in the culture has everything it needs, but the mature learner, operating at a distance from the culture, faces potentially lethal scarcity of the necessary cultural presentations. How can such a learner actually learn? The method I use of teaching students to be literate in a prose style consists of analyzing for them the cultural blending templates that define the style, in the hope of giving them a place to start. Then I invite them to spend all their time trying to enact the style on the fly. I discourage them from trying to revise their failures. I tell them that a prose style cannot be attained by tinkering with surface features and that any attempt to work in that fashion will produce only parody and finally paralysis. Besides, it's no fun. As you might expect, at the outset, my students often wonder how on earth they will learn what it is I have to teach, even what on earth I have to teach, but it works for me, and, to all appearances, for them. Many of their efforts are available in the student gallery of the Web presentation at ⟨http://www.classicprose.com⟩.

The research on conceptual integration suggests a number of lines for the development of foreign language teaching. First, an analysis of the grammar of a language consists principally—and for the adult foreign language learner almost entirely—of the presentation of the grammatical constructions available in the language to be deployed as cues to the mental construction of meaning. These constructions are blending templates that have been contrived by a culture. They have their own characteristic patterns of matching between input spaces, selective projection to the blend, and emergent meaning in the blend. It is plausible that the learner could acquire both the rudiments and the idiomatic nuances of constructions more rapidly and more surely by studying their blending templates and the relationships between them. In this respect, the theoretical analysis of integration networks might provide pedagogically useful instruments. It might provide principles of grammar that look less arbitrary. A textbook might include blending diagrams in the text, in the exercises, and in the appendix.

Second, research on conceptual integration might lead us to comparative cognitive study of languages in a manner reminiscent of traditional comparative grammars. The benefits of comparative analysis of similar constructions in related languages are evident for the theorist, but they might also be substantial for the learner.

And last, blending analysis applies not only to the grammar of a language but also to the styles that are available in that language. The foreign language learner typically wishes to learn both. A blending analysis can, at least in principle, present them in a unified manner.

Of course, a child does not learn his or her mother tongue by reading a book full of blending templates. He or she learns directly, immersed in the environment and in the use of the language. But the adult learner of a foreign language needs all the help he or she can get.

References

Fauconnier, G., and M. Turner. (1998). Conceptual Integration Networks. *Cognitive Science* 22(2): 133–87.

Goldberg, A. (1995). *Constructions: A Construction Grammar Approach to Argument Structure.* Chicago: University of Chicago Press.

Israel, M. (1996). The *Way* Constructions Grow. In *Conceptual Structure, Discourse, and Language,* edited by A. Goldberg, pp. 217–30. Stanford, Calif.: CSLI.

Mandelblit, N. (1995). Formal and Conceptual Blending in the Hebrew Verbal System: A Cognitive Basis for Verbal-Pattern Alternations in Modern Hebrew. Department of Cognitive Science, University of California at San Diego.

Reddy, M. (1979). The Conduit Metaphor. In *Metaphor and Thought,* edited by A. Ortony, pp. 284–324. Cambridge: Cambridge University Press.

Thomas, F.-N., and M. Turner. (1994). *Clear and Simple as the Truth: Writing Classic Prose.* Princeton: Princeton University Press.

Turner, M. (1996). *The Literary Mind: The Origins of Thought and Language.* New York: Oxford University Press.

——. (1999–). Web site: Blending and Conceptual Integration. ⟨http://blending.stanford .edu⟩.

Turner, M., and G. Fauconnier. (1999). A Mechanism of Creativity. *Poetics Today* 20 (3):397–418.

Turner, M., and F.-N. Thomas. (1998–). Web site: ⟨http://classicprose.com⟩.

3

Literacy as a New Organizing Principle for Foreign Language Education

RICHARD G. KERN

In their recent analysis of articles related to the teaching of literature published in *The Modern Language Journal* from 1916 to 1999, Kramsch and Kramsch (2000) identify the publication of the Coleman Report (Coleman 1929) as a pivotal moment that marked a dissociation of literacy from the study of literature. Whereas literature had traditionally been treated primarily in terms of its philological and aesthetic value, the focus of reading was now shifting toward what Kramsch and Kramsch characterize as a "literacy orientation" aimed at developing reading skills to access the informational content of texts. At the time, few literary scholars entered the debate spurred by the Coleman Report, leading Kramsch and Kramsch to observe that "Precisely at the historical juncture when the reading of texts could have brought the concerns of literary scholars and language teachers closer together, the gap was wider than it had ever been" (560).

This gap continues to exist today, commonly manifesting itself as a difference in goals, orientation, and methods between lower-division study (language) and upper-division study (literature). Introductory- and intermediate-level language teaching generally strives to promote communicative competence. But what is considered "communicative" has often been associated primarily with face-to-face, spoken communication. Although the best-known models of communicative competence, such as those of Canale (1983), Canale and Swain (1980), Savignon (1983), and Bachman (1990) certainly include written as well as oral discourse in their purview, the operationalization of the notion of communicative competence in textbooks and programs has tended to emphasize oral communication. Furthermore, there are ample instances in the professional literature that would appear to highlight speech in the definition of communicative competence. For example, although Hymes makes no effort to exclude written communication, he nevertheless has written, "I should therefore take *competence* as the most general term for the speaking and hearing capabilities of a person" (1971, p. 16). Terrell (1977) defined communicative competence as the ability to "understand the essential points of what a native speaker says to him in a real communication situation and can respond in such a way that the native speaker interprets the response with little or no effort and without errors that are so distracting that they interfere drastically with communication" (p. 326). Brown (1994) has defined communicative competence as "a dynamic, interpersonal construct that can only be examined by means of the overt performance of two or more individuals in the process of negotiating meaning" (p. 227). So although reading and writing are widely acknowledged as important skills, students tend to do relatively little genuine reading and writing (as opposed to reading and writing *practice*) before their advanced-level coursework. And what is considered competence tends to be strictly functional and performance-based (Can the student accurately comprehend key pieces of information? write a story in the past tense? provide supporting evidence for ideas?). There *is* an emphasis on meaning, but there is too seldom any systematic analysis of how particular meanings are created. In other words, relatively little attention is paid to the work of interpretation— and even less to the cultural bases of interpretation processes and communication practices.

As we stand at the threshold of the twenty-first century, the time is right to close the gap, to reunite literacy with literacy study in order to improve the coherence of language curricula. What this reuniting requires, however, is a reconceptualization of "literacy" such that both social and individual dimensions of written expression are explored, leading to language programs that value aesthetic as well as efferent reading (Rosenblatt 1978) and that teach students to know the difference.

What is called for is a reassessment of our priorities in teaching foreign languages at the college and university level. Broadly, I am arguing for a renewed and invigorated focus on written communication. In stating this desideratum I should clarify from the outset that I am not in any way suggesting that spoken communication should be de-emphasized. Quite the contrary. But in my experience it seems clear that learners cannot develop the kind of spoken communication ability required in academic settings without a serious commitment to the study of written communication, because much of the former for academic purposes requires "literate" sensibilities about the particular ways the foreign language can be used in written contexts. Oral communication also requires a familiarity with the cultural premises that underlie communication in another society, which, in the absence of lived experience in that society, are often discovered through texts.

Communicating successfully in another language means shifting frames of reference, shifting norms, shifting assumptions of what can and cannot be said, what has to be explicit and what should be tacit, and so forth. In other words, using another language effectively involves thinking differently about language and communication. The question is this: How can one begin to understand another way of thinking, how can one be sensitized to different cultural frames, when one is in a classroom far from where the language is spoken? One approach, and the one proposed in this chapter, is reading, writing, and discussing foreign language texts.

Writing and the visual media are the primary means by which we learn about and relate to past and present worlds outside our immediate community. When we examine the particular ways language is used to capture and express ideas and experiences, we not only learn a great deal about the conventions of the language—we also begin to glimpse the beliefs and values that underlie another people's uses of language.

Given that language learners in academic settings have limited opportunities to use the language, it is incumbent on educators to provide learners with the broadest and deepest exposure to the language that we can with the limited time we have available. Texts—written, oral, visual, audiovisual—offer learners new aesthetic experiences as well as content to interpret and critique. The point is not simply to give them something to talk about (content for the sake of practicing language) but to engage them in the thoughtful and creative act of making connections between grammar, discourse, meaning, between language and content, between language and culture, between another culture and their own—in short, making them aware of the webs, rather than strands, of meaning in human communication.

Recently there have been signs of renewed interest in the use of literature, stylistic analysis, and translation to promote language learning. This renewed interest is not merely a return to traditional grammar translation or to the early twentieth-century "reading method," which ultimately focused on mastering linguistic forms. Rather, it is a move to consider the importance, on one hand, of elements of individual expression such as style and point of view and, on the other, social dimensions of literary and nonliterary texts as expressions of cultural codes and ideological overtones. We are thus concerned with, as Paulo Freire (Freire and Macedo 1987) put it, reading the word and reading the world—and reading the world through the word.

Why "Literacy"?

"Literacy" is not a word commonly used in the context of foreign language teaching, and therefore some explanation of why I have chosen the word is in order. I use "literacy" to convey a broader scope than the terms "reading" and "writing" and to allow for a more unified discussion of relations between readers, writers, texts, culture, and language learning. When we focus on literacy, we consider reading and writing in their social contexts of use. We frame reading and writing as complementary dimensions of written communication—and so we focus on their interrelatedness rather than on their separateness as distinct skills.

There are two benefits to this perspective: first, it offers a broadened understanding of what reading and writing are, how they relate to one another, and how they are connected to other dimensions of language learning and language use; second, it offers a way to narrow the long-standing pedagogical gap that has traditionally divided what we do at the early levels of language teaching and what we do at the advanced levels. That is, it offers a way to reconcile the teaching of "communication" with the teaching of "textual analysis." And this reconciliation can potentially help us improve the degree of coherence across levels of the language curriculum.

That said, there is one significant disadvantage to using the word "literacy"—namely, that it is a noun. As we all know, the effect of nominalization is to transform processes into things. Our understanding of literacy has, in a sense, suffered at the hand of literacy's own devices—by virtue of its representation in written language. When we reify what is really a dynamic interaction of linguistic, cognitive, and social processes, we can be misled in how we understand—and how we teach—literacy.

Multiple Perspectives on Literacy

What, then, should we mean by "literacy"? The first thing one notices when one tries to define the term is that its meaning varies with time, place, and social context. Ostensibly literacy refers to reading and writing, but how it is characterized varies tremendously. Literacy can be viewed as a technique, as a set of language skills, as a set of cognitive abilities, as a group of social practices, or, as Deborah Brandt (1990) has put it, "a part of the highest human impulse to think and rethink experience in place" (p. 1). From a historical perspective, the meaning of literacy is also variable. Its etymological root, *litteratus*, referred to learnedness in Latin, but literacy has in certain periods simply referred to the ability to write one's own name.

From a cross-cultural perspective, the functions, values, and practices associated with literacy also vary significantly. What literacy means in working-class communities in rural South Carolina (Heath 1983) is not the same as what it means for the Vai people of Liberia (Scribner and Cole 1981), which is in turn quite different from what literacy is for Punjabis in London (Saxena 1994) or for Moroccans in Koranic schools (Wagner 1993). Consequently, a number of scholars have argued that it does not make any sense to talk about literacy as a monolithic phenomenon. Instead, we should be talking about *literacies* in the plural.

Research on literacy and literacies has expanded considerably in the past twenty years and is represented in disciplines as diverse as anthropology, history, education, rhetoric and composition, psychology, linguistics, and sociolinguistics. From this cross-disciplinary research a new general characterization is emerging. Literacy is construed as a collection of dynamic cultural processes, rather than as a static, monolithic set of psychological attributes. It is both public and private, both social and individual. It is about the creation and interpretation of meaning through texts, not just the ability to inscribe and decode written language. And it is "critical," involving a spirit of reflective skepticism.

This conception of literacy is not necessarily one to which language teachers widely subscribe. And it is certainly not how most language students think of literacy. What is more familiar is an understanding of reading and writing as separate skills to be practiced along with the skills of speaking and listening. Reading represents the skills involved in decoding words in order to get meaning, and writing represents the skills involved in putting words on paper in prescribed ways in order to produce meaning. This view, though of course partially true, tends to limit reading and writing to straightforward acts of information transfer. For many foreign language students, the de facto goal of reading is uncovering *the* meaning, *the* theme, *the* point of a text. That is to say, what the teacher reveals in class. Similarly, writing is all too often about capturing in *the* right words *the* summary or *the* analysis of something they have read.

Because our conceptions of literacy will inevitably influence how we teach reading and writing in the classroom (Farley 1995), it is essential to understand that literacy is more than a set of academic skills, more than inscribing and decoding words, and more than prescribed patterns of thinking. It is neither natural, nor universal, nor ideologically neutral, but culturally constructed. It is precisely because literacy is variable and intimately tied to sociocultural practices that it is so important in our teaching of language and culture.

Literacy in the Context of Foreign Language Teaching

Given this background, let us further explore the gap that divides language curricula by examining how literacy tends to be handled in academic foreign language programs.

At the lower levels of the curriculum, literacy tends to be viewed in terms of *basic skills.* Teaching is typically focused on correctness and convention, on one hand, and on *functional* activities (reading classified ads, weather reports, timetables, signs, menus, and so forth) on the other. Students also read short stories and journalistic texts, but the goal of this reading is often vocabulary and grammar practice rather than interpretation or aesthetic appreciation. Meaning tends to be treated as a property of the text and therefore to be deemed unproblematic once the reader has mastered the linguistic elements of the text. This *text-centric* view of literacy was clearly reflected, for example, in the 1980s version of the ACTFL Proficiency Guidelines for reading and writing, which dealt largely with text characteristics rather than what learners actually do when they read and write.

At the upper end of the curriculum, two additional strands of literacy come into play. One we could call the *high cultural* strand, which involves the transmission of cultural knowledge and the development of aesthetic appreciation, literary sensibility, and a cultivated spirit. The study of a particular literary canon, for example, is thought to foster this kind of literacy. The other strand, which we could call the *cognitive skills* strand, involves the development of textual analysis skills and critical thinking.

So, whereas the kind of literacy taught in introductory and intermediate courses is basically concerned with textual description, the kind taught in advanced courses is more analytical and critical. This shift in emphasis can contribute to a lack of articulation between introductory and advanced course work—a gap that can frustrate students and imperil enrollments in upper-division courses. The problem, however, extends beyond a mere shift in approach. It is ultimately tied to the way in which we tend to conceptualize literacy. In the context of foreign language education, the views of basic skills, high culture, and cognitive skills all share a number of important limitations.

First, they reify literacy as an end product of instruction instead of as a variable set of processes constrained by textual, cognitive, and social factors. As a result, teachers' efforts become oriented toward defining boundary lines of a minimum acceptable standard. How well do learners have to read and write (in general) to be considered functional? How many novels do they have to read, how many cultural "facts" do they have to absorb, to be deemed (culturally) literate? Which, and how many, analytical skills and strategies do they need to become (cognitively) literate? The problem comes when these arbitrary dividing lines, driven by public demands for accountability, define instructional objectives. Teachers may orient their teaching to the criterion measure of skills so they can demonstrate achievement of program goals, but students may remain at the periphery of literacy if they have not understood the relationship between skills and knowledge.

The second limitation is that these views of literacy tend to exclude contextual factors—how people in different communities produce and use texts in different ways. When educators see literacy primarily as an individual, "inside-the-head" phenomenon, they often disregard significant differences in the purposes, functions, and social value of literacy across cultural contexts. Such differences can cause cultural dissonance or clashes. For example, a Chinese ESL student who writes an essay incorporating sentences he has recalled verbatim from earlier reading may be accused of plagiarism, even though the scholarly tradition in which he has been trained may not construe it as such (Pennycook 1996). An American who is learning Arabic in Egypt and is not attuned to the shifts between standard and colloquial language in newspapers and political speeches may miss crucial clues to the writer's point of view. A Japanese ESL student schooled in the *yakudoku* tradition of reading as translation may encounter difficulties when she is asked to give a critical appraisal of an English text, because that request clashes with the classroom practices with which she is familiar (Hino 1992). So, instead of thinking of literacy as a single, generic, or readily transferable ability, we need to consider the question: *In what particular contexts, and for what particular purposes, can one be considered literate?*

The third limitation is that traditional views of literacy are largely incompatible with the goals of communicative language teaching, because they emphasize prescriptive norms rather than appropriateness of use. On one hand, we want our students to communicate effectively with different groups in a range of social contexts, using a variety of appropriate gambits in different situations. On the other, we teach—and most important, we test—a narrow standard of literacy that requires adherence to usage prescribed by a socially dominant norm. Moreover, this narrow standard tends to be increasingly reinforced and insisted on as one progresses through the levels of academic language study.

What is needed is a reconciliation between the emphasis on face-to-face verbal interaction and the development of learners' ability to read, discuss, think, and write critically about texts. These two sets of goals are not inherently incompatible. The challenge is to develop a conceptual framework that is broad enough to accommodate both of them. As a step in this direction, I propose a synthesis of these goals by enveloping the *textual* within a larger framework of the *communicative*—a framework that links, rather than divides, beginning and advanced levels of language learning. The groundwork for this move has been established over the past several decades, as an increasing number of notable language educators have argued for an emphasis on literacy in language teaching.

Calls for Foreign Language Literacy

In 1978, Henry Widdowson argued that *interpretation* underlies all communicative language abilities. Widdowson's scheme for developing learners' ability to discern the communicative value of texts (not simply their signification) relied on an integrated approach to reading and writing: "What the learner needs to know how to do," he argued, "is to compose in the act of writing, comprehend in the act of reading, and to learn techniques of reading by writing and techniques of writing by reading" (1978, p. 144).

Many of Widdowson's ideas were echoed and extended in two landmark books published in the 1990s: *Reading for Meaning* (1991) by Janet Swaffar, Katherine Arens, and Heidi Byrnes, and *Context and Culture in Language Teaching* (1993) by Claire Kramsch. Both books articulated a vision of foreign language education that shifted emphasis from sentence grammar, structure drills, and information retrieval to a more thoughtful mode of learning that involved students' reflection on language and content and specifically on the connections between the details of texts and students' personal responses to those texts.

Other foreign language educators have added their voices. Marlies Mueller (1991) argues that students need to be made aware of how systems of interpretation are historically created and how they vary with time and place. She recommends the teaching of a "pluralistic literacy" that introduces students to "diverse ways of reading that will enable them to recognize the political and moral implications of diverse ways of understanding" (p. 22).

Similarly, Russell Berman (1996) has called for "foreign cultural literacy" as a pedagogical goal that entails "a student's familiarity with and facility in the language, values, and narratives of a culture not his or her own" (p. 43). According to Berman, foreign cultural literacy would highlight the interplay between language and culture and familiarize students not only with the literary canon but also with the "stories another culture tells about itself" (p. 43), as reflected in films, songs, status symbols, political discourse, and everyday language.

Focusing on the often-difficult transition from language study to literary study at the second-year college level, Richard Jurasek (1996) sees literacy as a key concept for curricular integration. He has proposed an intermediate-level language curriculum that incorporates what he calls literacy-related "inquiry subsets." These involve exploring cultures as perceptual systems and using texts to heighten students' awareness of how we construct meaning.

Finally, Heidi Byrnes (1998) has recently developed a remarkable literacy-based curriculum in the German Department at Georgetown University. She argues that designing a curriculum around literacy makes it easier to integrate the teaching of language, literary interpretation, and culture.

Although the details of their proposals differ somewhat, Widdowson, Swaffar, Kramsch, Mueller, Berman, Jurasek, and Byrnes all see reading and writing not as peripheral support skills but as a crucial hub where language, culture, and thought converge. They argue for systematically guiding learners in their efforts to create, interpret, and reflect on discourse in order to better understand how meanings are made and received, both in their own culture and in another.

Principles of a Sociocognitive View of Literacy

As a starting point in considering a literacy-based approach to language teaching, I have proposed a working definition for an expanded notion of literacy that weaves together linguistic, cognitive, and sociocultural strands. This definition is not meant to describe all forms of literacy but rather to characterize literacy in the specific context of academic foreign language education.

Literacy is the use of socially, historically, and culturally situated practices of creating and interpreting meaning through texts. It entails at least a tacit awareness of the relations between textual conventions and their contexts of use and, ideally, the ability to reflect critically on those relations. Because it is purpose-sensitive, literacy is dynamic—not static—and variable across and within discourse communities and cultures. It draws on a wide range of cognitive abilities, on knowledge of written and spoken language, on knowledge of genres, and on cultural knowledge (Kern 2000, p. 16).

This definition is admittedly fairly abstract. In order to establish more useful guidelines for teaching practice, we can consider seven principles that emerge from this definition that can be applied concretely to language teaching.

1. Literacy involves interpretation. Writers and readers participate in double acts of interpretation—the writer interprets the world (experiences, events, ideas, and so on), and the reader in turn interprets the writer's interpretation in terms of his or her own conception of the world.

2. Literacy involves collaboration. Writers write for an audience, even if they write only for themselves. Their decisions about what needs to be said and what can go without saying are based on their understanding of their audience. Readers, in turn, must contribute their motivation, knowledge, and experience in order to make the writer's text meaningful.

3. Literacy involves conventions. How people read and write texts is not universal, but is governed by cultural conventions that evolve through use and are modified for individual purposes.

4. Literacy involves cultural knowledge. Reading and writing function within particular systems of attitudes, beliefs, customs, ideals, and values. Readers and writers that are operating from outside a given cultural system risk misunderstanding, or being misunderstood by, people who are operating on the inside of the cultural system.

5. Literacy involves problem solving. Because words are always embedded in linguistic and situational contexts, reading and writing involve figuring out relationships between words, between larger units of meaning, and between texts and real or imagined worlds.

6. Literacy involves reflection and self-reflection. Readers and writers think about language and its relations to the world and themselves.

7. Literacy involves language use. Literacy is not just about writing systems, nor is it just about lexical and grammatical knowledge. It requires knowledge of how language is used in spoken, as well as written, contexts to create discourse. (Kern 2000, pp. 16–17)

Although I have framed these principles in terms of reading and writing, they are not unique to literacy and apply broadly to communication in general. In fact, the seven principles might be summarized by a macro-principle: literacy involves communication. This seven-point linkage between literacy and communication has important implications for language teaching, since it provides a bridge to span the gap that all too often separates introductory *communicative* language teaching and advanced *literary* teaching.

The seven principles of literacy as communication provide some guidance in identifying what and how to teach in order to support a general goal of reflective communication. *Language, conventions,* and *cultural knowledge* form the basic elements to be taught, and they are taught in conjunction with the processes of *interpretation, collaboration, problem solving,* and *reflection.* These elements and processes can be taught using a variety of activities that, as a group, address four different but complementary literacy needs of the foreign language learner: (1) to be immersed meaningfully in written language; (2) to receive direct assistance in the complexities of reading and writing FL texts; (3) to learn to analyze and evaluate what they read; and (4) to learn how to transform meanings into new representations. Although space does not permit me to demonstrate the concrete application of the seven principles to the teaching of a text, the reader is referred to Kern (2000) for multiple detailed examples. What is important to clarify, however, is that there is no dogmatic *method* associated with literacy-based teaching. Rather, learners' needs can be addressed using a wide variety of instructional activities already familiar to language teachers, such as voluntary reading, readers' theater, reading journals, free writing, semantic mapping, discussions based on critical focus questions, textual comparisons, translation, summary writing, stylistic pastiches, and other kinds of textual reformulations.

Goals of a Literacy-Based Curriculum

How do the goals of literacy-based teaching compare with our previous goals? Literacy-based teaching assumes the primary importance of developing communicative ability in a new language, but it also emphasizes within that general goal the development of learners' ability to analyze, interpret, and transform discourse, to think critically about how discourse is constructed and how it is used toward various social ends. In other words, it emphasizes both oral and written communication that is informed by a metacommunicative awareness of how discourse is derived from relations between language use, contexts of interaction, and larger sociocultural contexts.

So, a literacy-based curriculum is neither a purely structural nor a purely communicative approach; rather, it attempts to relate communicative and structural dimensions of language use, as illustrated in table 3.1.

Adopting literacy as an organizing principle of language teaching entails

Table 3.1 Goals of Structural, Communicative, and Literacy-Based Curricula

Structural Emphasis	Communicative Emphasis	Literacy Emphasis
Knowing	Doing	Doing and reflecting on doing in terms of knowing
Usage	Use	Usage-use relations
Language forms	Language functions	Form-function relations
Achievement (display of knowledge)	Functional ability to communicate	Communicative appropriateness informed by metacommunicative awareness

Source: Kern 2000, p. 304.

subtle but important changes in teaching and curriculum. Instructional objectives shift from an emphasis on conversation for conversation's sake or the delivery of linguistic and cultural facts toward the development of learners' ability to interpret and evaluate critically language use in a variety of spoken and written contexts. Instructional activities (such as those listed above) emphasize interdependencies among speaking, listening, reading, and writing skills and focus students' attention on the interactions between linguistic form, situational context, and communicative and expressive functions. The study of language and the study of literature are treated as mutually dependent, not mutually exclusive, activities.

A literacy-based curriculum, by including nonliterary texts, may at first blush seem to deprivilege literature. This perception is valid to the extent that the focus of instruction is broadened beyond an *exclusive* focus on literary texts. The value of literary study, however, is ultimately enhanced, not diminished, because textuality becomes a major focus of teaching at all levels. Explicit links can be made between literary writing and other forms of cultural expression, such as film, art, music, architecture, and news media, thus improving students' understanding of how literature fits into the "big picture" of signifying practices in the foreign society. Time spent on the exploration of cultural narratives in various popular media might displace time spent on the next literary text on the syllabus, but if such digressions serve to illuminate students' understanding of certain cultural underpinnings of that literary text and create a bridge to what students are learning in their culture or civilization courses, then it is time well spent. As students begin to understand the connections between different forms of cultural expression, their interest and motivation to study literature will likely increase significantly.

Although it is not possible to explore the features of a literacy-based curriculum in great detail here (again, the reader is referred to Kern 2000), two key features are noteworthy: (1) the way in which reading, writing, and discussion are sequenced in the classroom and (2) the new respective roles of students and teachers.

Sequencing of Instruction

In the traditional foreign language curriculum, reading, talking, and writing are relatively distinct phases of a linear instructional sequence. Students generally prepare for class by reading a text. They talk about the text in class, and then they are sometimes asked to write an essay about it. Sometimes students write notes or keep a reading journal, in which case the sequence bypasses discussion. Talking sometimes precedes reading, as in pre-reading activities. Rarely, however, does writing precede either reading or talking. The phases are typically discrete and sequential, rather than recursive, as shown in figure 3.1. Most often that which *can* be done outside of class (that is, reading and writing) is, in order to reserve class time for talking. This makes talking the primary collaborative activity and maintains reading and writing as activities that students do mainly on their own.

The problem with the traditional sequence of instruction is that students get little direct help with what they typically report to be the most difficult part of language study, namely, reading and writing. It is quite possible, in fact, that reading and writing are so often perceived as difficult precisely *because* they are so often done outside of class, by oneself, alone. If they were more often brought into the mainstream of classroom activity, if they were made to be collaborative as well as individual activities, they would perhaps not seem so difficult.

For example, reading to identify thematic elements of a text or to identify its underlying assumptions or ideological bias are not well-practiced habits for most students. In fact, learners often need to be shown what teachers mean by these things before they can do what they have been asked to do. In other words, simply handing students a text to read is often not enough; teachers need to start off by leading students to recognize the kinds of textual phenomena they hope students will ultimately recognize on their own when they read. First and foremost, this usually requires engaging learners in discussion—or writing—*before* they read. In literacy-based teaching the relation between reading, writing and talking is not linear but overlapping, as shown in figure 3.2.

It is the overlap that most clearly differentiates a literacy-focused curricu-

Fig. 3.1. Traditional Linear Relationship of Reading, Talking, and Writing

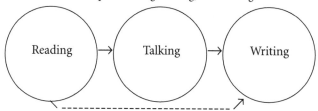

Source: Kern 2000, p. 131.

lum from traditional curricula. Reading and writing overlap not only in the sense that students write formal essays about what they've read. They also overlap

- when students use writing to concretely represent their thoughts and interpretations of texts as they read—in the form of reading journals, summaries, diagrams, and so forth;
- when students write their own version of a topic or a theme *before* reading the target text, in order to be sensitized to the topic or theme before reading commences;
- when students write reflections on their own reading processes—their experiences, difficulties, and insights—as a component of their reports on their independent reading;
- when students read to improve their writing—when they attend to linguistic, rhetorical, or stylistic elements in texts in order to incorporate them into their own writing; and
- when students actively and critically read their own and their peers' writing in the editing process.

Working in these areas of overlap can not only bridge the traditional divisions among the so-called four skills of speaking, listening, reading and writing but can also help bridge the gap that too often separates the teaching of language from the teaching of literature.

Roles of Teachers and Learners

Another general feature of a literacy-based curriculum has to do with the roles that teachers and students play. These roles have been linked for a long time to the notion of apprenticeship. What has changed is the focus of the apprenticeship. In the days of grammar translation and later structural or audiolingual language teaching methods, students were apprentices to

Fig. 3.2. The Relation of Reading, Writing, and Talking in a Literacy-Based Curriculum

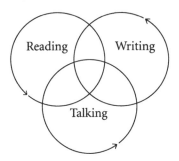

Source: Kern 2000, p. 132.

philologists or linguists. The communicative competence models of the 1980s made the native speaker the model, and students often apprenticed with the ultimate aim of developing "near-native" competence. In literacy-based language teaching, students are aiming to become neither apprentice philologists nor apprentice native speakers but rather apprentice discourse analysts and intercultural explorers.

One of the biggest challenges is establishing teacher and student roles that allow for critical analysis of classroom communication itself. The role that typified structural approaches to language teaching (and one that is still often expected by students) is that of the traditional authority: the teacher is the one who is always right, the one who has the knowledge the students need to acquire, the one who manages and controls everything that happens in the classroom. This role tends to polarize responsibility for learning. If the students do not learn, it is either because the teacher did not teach things right or because the students are too lazy or not smart enough. The learner role that complements an authoritative teacher role is one of deference and relative passivity.

A more contemporary teacher role, born of communicative, "learner-centered" language teaching, is represented by the well-known motto "The teacher is the guide on the side, not the sage on the stage." The idea is that the teacher designs and organizes learning activities and then gets out of the way, so that students can go about their business of communicating and learning. Responsibility for what happens in the class (including student learning) is therefore shared: the teacher is there to organize, to motivate, to provide assistance and feedback, but the students must play an active participatory role that involves a considerable degree of autonomy in the form of self-motivation, self-direction, and cooperation.

Unfortunately, neither of these sets of roles is likely to promote the kind of classroom culture that fosters critical thinking and metacommunicative awareness. What is needed to accomplish these goals is a recasting of teacher and learner roles inherited from structural and communicative approaches. This recasting is linked to what I call the three R's of literacy-based teaching, namely, Responding, Revising, and Reflecting.

Responding

Responding means both "giving a reply" and "reacting." Both meanings come into play when we read, write, and talk. When we read, we respond in the "reacting" sense, based on how well what we are reading meshes with our knowledge, beliefs, values, attitudes, and so on. We also respond in the "replying" sense when we fill in discourse that the writer has left implicit in the text. Furthermore, during the process of talking about a text, the various responses put forth by students and the teacher become "secondary texts" to which one also responds—and these secondary responses will ultimately influence one's response to the primary, written text.

Writing involves responding in both concrete and abstract ways. On the concrete level, we respond to a letter, to an assignment, or to an exam question by writing. On a more abstract level, the processes of inventing, planning, redesigning, and evaluating what we want to say involve responding to a complex array of factors, including the task demands, the ultimate purpose of the writing, and the identity of the addressee. From this abstract perspective, every text that students write is a response, as is every text they read. A literacy-based approach to teaching thus encourages students not only to respond to the texts they read but also to have some sense of how those texts are themselves responses to something.

Revising

Revising is often associated exclusively with writing. In literacy-based teaching, though, revision is an important part of a wide range of activities. At the level of the lesson plan, as well as at the level of curriculum, literacy-based teaching emphasizes rereading, rewriting, rethinking, reframing, and redesigning language. The point is not to repeat but to redo within a different contextual frame, with a different purpose, or for a different audience, in order to develop students' ability to reflect on how they design meaning differently in diverse situations.

Rereading is a way to fine-tune interpretations and make connections that were not at first obvious, but it is also a way to better understand the reading process itself. When readers can evaluate their responses to reading from various angles, they can experience the ways meaning can shift as contexts of interpretation change. If readers are bound to a view of reading as remembering as much as possible from a single pass through a text, they not only limit the richness of their reading experience but also hold themselves back from fully developing their communicative potential as language users.

Writing, of course, benefits considerably from revision. What is most significant from a language teaching perspective is not the quality of the final draft but the effects of the revising process itself on the stance that learners take toward their writing, the kinds of questions they ask themselves, and their capacity to reshape their expression—and perhaps even their intentions.

The teacher plays an important role in providing specific purposes for revision. Simply giving students more time to read or write will probably not be enough. Students need some kind of structure—like comparing one draft or reading with another, but *with a specific purpose in making the comparison.* The purpose might come from class discussion, or it might come from students' journals. Most often it will need to be specified by the teacher.

Students' speaking ability can also be enhanced by revision and redesigning. One student's telling of a story can be developed into a series of retellings that allow students to express and experience multiple meanings based on the same content. When the teacher systematically varies the parameters of context, students can become aware of the relations between language, context, and meaning.

Reflecting

The third R, reflecting, has to do with evaluation. From the standpoint of receptive language use (that is, listening, reading, viewing), reflecting might involve questions like the following: What might be this person's intentions? What does this particular manner of expression imply about the speaker's or the writer's beliefs and attitudes about the topic, about me (the reader or listener), and about our relation to one another? Are other signs (body language, gestures, situational context, text formatting) consistent with what has been said or written? or do they somehow modify the meaning?

From the standpoint of expressive language use (that is, speaking and writing), reflecting might involve questions like the following: In what ways might the other person interpret what I say if I say it like this? What am I assuming about his or her knowledge or beliefs? Is it appropriate for me to say this, given who I am in relation to my interlocutor or reader?

Tied up in all of these questions are issues of cultural norms and cultural

Table 3.2 Summary of Teacher-Learner Roles in Structural, Communicative, and Literacy-Based Curricula

	Structural Emphasis	Communicative Emphasis	Literacy Emphasis
Role models for teachers and learners	philologists or linguists	native speakers	discourse analysts and intercultural explorers
Primary mode of teacher response	Correcting (enforcing a prescriptive norm)	Responding (to communicative intent)	Responding (to language as used), focusing attention on reflection and revision
Predominant learner roles	Deference to authority: focus on absorption and analysis of material presented	Active participation: focus on using language in face-to-face interaction	Active engagement: focus on using language, reflecting on language use, and revising

Source: Adapted from Kern 2000, p. 312.

knowledge. In reflecting on culture, teachers need to be concerned not only with the target culture to which learners are being exposed but also with the culture or cultures that learners themselves bring to the language classroom and the relation between the two. The culture that learners (and teachers) bring to the foreign language classroom is more than just a background influence. It shapes everything that happens in the classroom, including how teachers and students interact and how they evaluate one another's roles and performance.

When we acknowledge the importance of learners' agency in the meaning-making process and the cultural values inherent in language use, our teaching gains greater currency in an international framework. We not only promote deeper understanding of the language but also equip learners to uncover the cultural frames surrounding language use, perhaps long past the point when their formal language study has ended.

We can summarize the shifts in teacher and learner roles corresponding to the goals set out earlier, situating the three R's of responding, revising, and reflecting in relation to roles emphasized in structural and communicative approaches, in table 3.2.

Conclusion

Reading and writing are the most powerful modes of formal learning. They are fundamental to intellectual inquiry and creativity in all disciplines. I have suggested that the language teaching profession consider an approach to teaching that frames reading and writing as highly interrelated acts of communication that are not only relevant for those with literary aspirations but essential for *all* language learners and at *all* levels of language study.

The approach I am advocating is one that is focused on relationships: linguistic, cognitive, and social relationships between readers, writers, texts, and culture; between form and meaning; between reading and writing; and between spoken and written communication. By organizing foreign language teaching around literacy, we assert the importance of textual analysis; we also emphasize the need to widen the scope of inquiry beyond the literary canon to include a range of written and spoken texts that broadly represents the particular signifying practices of a society. Moreover, we focus on providing learners with structured guidance in the thinking that goes into reading, writing, and speaking appropriately in particular contexts.

This emphasis on thinking in a literacy-based curriculum blurs the traditional division between language skills and academic content because language use itself becomes an object of reflection and thus constitutes a source of intellectual content. For the reasons I have outlined in this chapter, I believe that an integrated focus on the linguistic, cognitive, and social dimensions of literacy can help us close the language-literature gap and ultimately enhance the coherence of language teaching and learning at all levels of study.

References

Bachman, L. F. (1990). *Fundamental Considerations in Language Testing.* Oxford: Oxford University Press.

Berman, R. A. (1996). Reform and Continuity: Graduate Education Toward a Foreign Cultural Literacy. *ADFL Bulletin* 27(3): 40–46.

Brandt, D. (1990). *Literacy as Involvement: The Acts of Writers, Readers, and Texts.* Carbondale: Southern Illinois University Press.

Brown, H.D. (1994). *Principles of Language Learning and Teaching,* 3d ed. Englewood Cliffs, N.J.: Prentice-Hall Regents.

Byrnes, H. (1998). Constructing Curricula in Collegiate Foreign Language Departments. In *Learning Foreign and Second Languages: Perspectives in Research and Scholarship,* edited by H. Byrnes, pp. 262–95. New York: Modern Language Association.

Canale, M. (1983). From Communicative Competence to Communicative Language Pedagogy. In *Language and Communication,* edited by J. C. Richards and R. W. Schmidt, pp. 2–27. London: Longman.

Canale, M., and M. Swain. (1980). Theoretical Bases of Communicative Approaches to Second Language Teaching and Testing. *Applied Linguistics* 1(1): 1–47.

Coleman, A. (1929). *The Teaching of Modern Foreign Languages.* New York: Macmillan.

Farley, T. (1995). *An Ethnographic Study of Two College Teachers' Beliefs About Reading in the Introductory Foreign Language Literature Class.* Ph.D. diss., Indiana University.

Freire, P., and Macedo, D. (1987). *Literacy: Reading the Word and the World.* South Hadley, Mass.: Bergin and Garvey.

Heath, S. B. (1983). *Ways with Words: Ethnography of Communication in Communities and Classroom.* New York: Cambridge University Press.

Hino, N. (1992). The *Yakudoku* Tradition of Foreign Language Literacy in Japan. In *Cross-Cultural Literacy: Global Perspectives on Reading and Writing,* edited by F. Dubin and N. A. Kuhlman, pp. 99–111. Englewood Cliffs, N.J.: Prentice-Hall Regents.

Hymes, D. (1971). Competence and Performance in Linguistic Theory. In *Language Acquisition: Models and Methods,* edited by R. Huxley and E. Ingram, pp. 3–28. London: Academic.

Jurasek, R. (1996). Intermediate-Level Foreign Language Curricula: An Assessment and a New Agenda. *ADFL Bulletin* 27(2): 18–27.

Kern, R. G. (2000). *Literacy and Language Teaching.* Oxford: Oxford University Press.

Kramsch, C. (1993). *Context and Culture in Language Teaching.* Oxford: Oxford University Press.

Kramsch, C., and O. Kramsch. (2000). The Avatars of Literature in Language Study. *Modern Language Journal* 84(4): 553–73.

Mueller, M. (1991). Cultural Literacy and Foreign Language Pedagogy. *ADFL Bulletin* 22(2): 19–24.

Pennycook, A. (1996). Borrowing Others' Words: Text, Ownership, Memory, and Plagiarism. *TESOL Quarterly* 30(2): 201–30.

Rosenblatt, L. M. (1978). *The Teacher, the Text, the Poem: The Transactional Theory of the Literary Work.* Carbondale: Southern Illinois University Press.

Savignon, S. J. (1983). *Communicative Competence: Theory and Classroom Practice.* Reading, Mass.: Addison-Wesley.

Saxena, M. (1994). Literacies Among the Punjabis in Southall. In *Worlds of Literacy,* edited by M. Hamilton and D. Barton and R. Ivanic, pp. 195–214. Clevedon, U.K.: Multilingual Matters.

Scribner, S., and M. Cole. (1981). *The Psychology of Literacy.* Cambridge: Harvard University Press.

Swaffar, J. K., K. M. Arens, and H. Byrnes. (1991). *Reading for Meaning: An Integrated Approach to Language Learning.* Englewood Cliffs, N.J.: Prentice-Hall.

Terrell, T. D. (1977). A Natural Approach to Second Language Acquisition and Learning. *Modern Language Journal* 61(7): 325–37.

Wagner, D. A. (1993). *Literacy, Culture, and Development: Becoming Literate in Morocco.* Cambridge: Cambridge University Press.

Widdowson, H. G. (1978). *Teaching Language as Communication.* Oxford: Oxford University Press.

4

Playing Games with Literacy: The Poetic Function in the Era of Communicative Language Teaching

CARL BLYTH

The literacy events of my college French class, a third-semester course, are the standard fare of today's so-called communicatively oriented classroom: deciphering menus, skimming train schedules, analyzing polling data, scanning newspaper headlines, and so on. In contrast to my French classroom's reality-based texts, the bedtime stories I read to my young daughter are concerned with imaginary worlds. *The Cat in the Hat* is one of our all-time favorites. With nonsensical words, catchy rhymes, and silly characters, Dr. Seuss keeps us thoroughly entertained.

As if this juxtaposition of literacy contexts had not given me enough food for thought, two recent experiences left me pondering the nature of literacy in beginning foreign language classrooms. The first occurred during my foreign language methods class. I had asked my students to analyze the way the *passé composé*, a French compound past tense, was presented in eight different first-year textbooks. The textbooks, all top sellers in the first-year market, are printed and distributed by the major publishers: McGraw-Hill, Heinle & Heinle, and Holt, Rinehart and Winston, among others. I was surprised to discover that none included the famous poem "Déjeuner du Matin" by Jacques Prévert, once considered part of the pedagogical canon of the French language curriculum. The disappearance of Prévert's poem illustrates a continuing trend in the publishing of pedagogical foreign language materials: poetry, song, and literary texts have gradually given way to informational texts and various forms of realia.

The second experience was an unsettling conversation I had with a very talented and creative teaching assistant, a French women who held a master's degree in foreign language education from the Sorbonne. One day during a doctoral seminar in research methods, I asked the teaching assistant about the research that she had conducted as part of her master's program. She told me that she had experimented with the use of songs in her classrooms and had come to believe that music held great potential for foreign language learning. Assuming that she had continued to use songs in her French classes at the University of Texas, I asked her which ones seemed to work best with American students. My question seemed to take her by surprise. Choosing her words carefully, she answered that she had not used any songs since beginning to teach in the United States. When I asked why she had not continued the practice, she explained that the use of songs did not conform to the dominant communicative methodologies in American universities. Her comments made me wonder if other talented instructors had decided to forgo pedagogical practices out of fear that they might not conform to our program's "communicative" methodology!

As a foreign language educator, teacher trainer, and language program director, I have often participated in discussions in which the elusive and polyvalent word "communicative" is used to trump all competing pedagogical practices. I am frankly worried that many teachers who have embraced communicative language teaching (however they may define it) hold questionable beliefs about communication. I contend that the belief systems of many teachers who define their approach to language teaching as "communicative," "interactional," "task-based," "process-oriented," "procedural," or "learner centered" often reduce communication to what is known as referential or transactional language. In an insightful article titled "Language Play, Language Learning," the applied linguist Guy Cook notes the existence of two underlying premises of communicative language teaching (CLT):

> *First premise:* Authentic/natural language is best for language learning.
> *Second premise:* Authentic/natural language is primarily practical and purposeful, focused upon meaning rather than form.
>
> (Cook 1997, p. 224)

Cook begins by questioning the meaning of the terms *natural* and *authentic*. The two terms are more or less synonymous, and though rarely defined by their advocates, they appear to refer to language used in so-called ordinary conversation between adult native speakers. Yet in practice these terms are simply modifiers that indicate approval rather than any intrinsic quality. Cook compares the phrase "natural language" to such vacuous advertising terms as "natural sweetness" and "natural goodness." If *natural* and *authentic* define a type of language, then presumably they must have opposites. What then is *inauthentic* or *unnatural* language? Many advocates of CLT disdain pedagogical texts because they are "doctored," that is, they contain a purposely simplified grammar. But Cook points out that simplified syntax and lexis are to be expected in certain natural contexts, for example, when adults address children or when native speakers address nonnative speakers. "What could be more unnatural and unauthentic than teachers trying to force themselves—against their better instincts—to talk to language learners as they talk to their compatriots?" (Cook 1997, p. 225). Cook's arguments remind educators that the classroom has its own authenticity. Coining the term "authentic artifice," Cook quotes VanLier, who claims that pedagogically contrived texts are often perceived to be authentic by the learner: "In a curious way it seems to me that the traditional language lessons of the grammar translation type which I remember from my school days might lay greater claim to that sort of authenticity than some of the so-called communicative classrooms that I have had occasion to observe in recent years. I must emphasize that the old lessons seem to have been authentic for me, although they may well have been inauthentic for some of my classmates" (VanLier 1996, p. 128). And then there is the rather obvious point that in language teaching, as in life in general, even if a clear distinction between the natural and the artificial could be established, there is no necessary correlation between what is natural and what is desirable. As Cook sums up: "Many bad aspects of human behavior are natural ones: and many good ones are unnatural" (p. 226).

In this chapter I argue for the importance of the poetic function for language acquisition and thus challenge the two underlying premises of CLT described by Cook. The term "poetic function" was coined by the Russian linguist and literary theorist Roman Jakobson (1960). Following Jakobson's work, I show that the poetic function is not a marginal function confined to literary genres. Rather, it is present in most forms of communication to varying degrees. I contend that proponents of CLT often reduce communication to strictly referential language—the exchange of new information regarding the context. I argue that such a reductionist view of communication has had harmful consequences for our foreign language curricula. I conclude by calling for the resurrection of the poetic function in beginning and intermediate foreign language classrooms.

The Purpose of Communication

Before discussing the poetic function and its uses in the language class-room, it is imperative to examine how proponents of CLT conceive of the purposes of communication. In the influential foreign language teaching methods textbook *Making Communicative Language Teaching Happen* (Lee and VanPatten 1995), the authors summarize the purposes of communication as follows:

> In the non-classroom world, people engage in communication for a variety of reasons. However, the two most common purposes of communication can be described as psychosocial and informational-cognitive. The psychosocial purpose of language involves using language to bond socially or psychologically with someone or some group or to engage in social behavior in some way. Thus, asking someone "How's it going?" might be less a desire to know the actual details of someone's life than a means of exchanging pleasantries or letting someone know that you care. The informational-cognitive use of language involves communication for the purpose of obtaining information, generally for some other task. . . .
>
> What of the language classroom? While the instructor may use language for both psychosocial and informational-cognitive purposes, it is doubtful that the learner, especially in the beginning and intermediate stages, would use language for many psychosocial purposes. The classroom context typically does not promote the kind of interaction that requires language to be used psychosocially. The classroom, however, does lend itself exceptionally well to the use of communicative language for informational-cognitive purposes. The classroom is ideally suited to the development and implementation of activities in which learners exchange information for a common purpose. (pp. 150–51)

According to Cook (2000), most proponents of CLT share Lee's and Van-Patten's assumption that the overriding purpose of communication is the exchange of information about the context, that is, information that is either ostensibly true or false. Cook contends that an educator who holds such a view of communication will logically be compelled to "create classroom language use which is needs-based, meaning-focused, 'real,' and culturally conventional" (p. 149).

In contrast to the widespread belief that the purpose of communication is essentially referential, Roman Jakobson maintained that reference was but one function of the many purposes of communication. According to Caton (1987), Jakobson and the Prague School maintained that "Reference is not the only, nor even the primary goal of communication" (cited in Waugh and

Monville-Burston 1990, p. 15). According to Jakobson, language was best conceived of as a system of systems suited to various communicative goals. In his presidential address at the annual meeting of the Linguistic Society of America in 1956, Jakobson presented for the first time his typology of the speech event and the corresponding communicative functions. He schematized the speech event as involving six essential factors: the speaker, the addressee, the context, the message (utterance), the contact, and the code. Each of these six factors corresponds to a different function of language. In other words, verbal messages have various meanings or functions that can be described in terms of their "set" (*Einstellung*) toward one of these six factors. Jakobson believed that the various functions were amenable to analysis because they relied on conventionalized linguistic signs.

The Speech Event and the Corresponding Functions

context (referential)
message (poetic)
speaker (emotive)   addressee (conative)
contact (phatic)
code (metalingual)
(Waugh and Monville-Burston 1990, p. 16)

According to this schema, if the message is focused on the context, its primary function is said to be *referential,* also variously called *cognitive, denotative,* or *informational.* Although reference may be the leading task of many—perhaps most—messages, Jakobson repeatedly stressed the importance of the other functions for communication. The *emotive* function focuses on the speaker's emotional state. The purely emotive stratum of language is best exemplified by interjections, which differ from the means of referential language both in their sound pattern and in their syntactic role. Different interjections signal different emotional states of the speaker: Damn it! All right! Whoa! Jakobson termed an orientation toward the addressee the *conative* function, which finds its purest grammatical expression in the vocative and the imperative. For example, if a teacher became annoyed at a talkative student, she might say, "Please be quiet!" Such an utterance cannot be challenged in terms of whether it is true. On the other hand, a referential, declarative statement about the context such as "The young man in the back row is not paying attention to the lesson" is open to contradiction.

The *phatic* function of language serves to establish contact between the speaker and the audience or listener. In other words, speakers routinely attempt to draw the attention of the interlocutor and confirm his or her attention ("Eh?" "Right?"). Conversely, listeners frequently signal that they are attending to the message ("Uh-huh," "Mm-hm"). Phatic communication is present in all small talk, a form of conversation in which information that is well known or obvious to both parties is expressed. Jackobson cites an eloquent example from the satirist Dorothy Parker:

> "Well!" the young man said.
> "Well!" she said.
> "Well, here we are," he said.
> "Here we are," she said, "Aren't we?"
> "I should say we were!" he said.
> "Eeyop! Here we are. Well!" she said.
> "Well," he said, "well."
> (cited in Waugh and Monville-Burston 1990, p. 75)

These ritualized formulas are meant to initiate and sustain the communication, to maintain contact, nothing more. (Of course, in the case of Parker's piece, one doubts whether the conversation will ever progress beyond the phatic!)

Well known to language teachers, the *metalingual* function is the use of language to refer to language. Whenever someone asks the meaning of a word or utterance, the metalingual function predominates. The interdiction of explicit grammar explanation, common to most "natural" approaches, aims to avoid the metalingual function, which is found to be suspect by some language learning theorists ("Teachers should not waste time talking about the language: they should speak the language.") But, in fact, Jakobson contended that first as well as second language learning is characterized by the metalingual function, or what is now commonly referred to in the jargon of the day as "the negotiation of meaning." After all, nothing could be more natural than for a language learner to ask questions about the grammar and vocabulary when he or she struggles to comprehend an utterance or text.

The *poetic* function of language occurs whenever there is a focus on the formal elements of a message—the phonological, morphological, syntactic, semantic, and discursive forms. Literary scholars commonly discuss the poetic function in terms of figures of speech and rhetorical devices; more specifically, they analyze alliteration, repetition, rhyme, meter, punning, metaphor, imagery, and so on. As an example of the poetic function, Jakobson cites the political slogan "I like Ike," three monosyllables that repeat the same diphthong *ay* set off by the consonants *l* and *k*. Equivalent slogans such as "*I like Reagan,*" "*I like Bush,*" or "*I like Clinton*" all fall flat, because, in part, of the lack of the poetic function.

According to Jakobson, the poetic function was not only to be found in poetry but in all forms of communication. Inspired by the work of Jakobson, Deborah Tannen has demonstrated that quintessentially literary devices are prevalent in everyday talk (Tannen 1987, 1989). Her main point is that although "ordinary" conversation may be predominantly referential in function, the poetic function is always present, as evidenced by patterns of repetition and parallelism.

Language Learning

So what does the poetic function have to do with language learning and second language literacy? Nearly all language acquisition specialists have remarked on the intensely poetic nature of child language (Kuczaj 1983; Owens 1996). One of the most commonplace observations in the psycholinguistic literature is that young children repeat utterances addressed to them without any recognition of the referential value of the words (Kuczaj 1983). They seem to be captured by formal properties of the language, under the spell of the sounds, as it were. Children produce utterances well before they understand the referential function of the spoken word. These nonreferential utterances seem to privilege the phatic function (establishing and prolonging contact with the caregiver) and the poetic function (creation of language for aesthetic reasons). Child language does not have to have a purpose in the sense of completing a task. It is not necessarily a means to an end. Rather, it seems that for children language production is a pleasurable end in itself.

Guy Cook makes the connections between language play, language learning, and a focus on linguistic form even more explicit. In a direct challenge to CLT's second premise, he claims:

"Far from being fixated on meaningful language to effect social action (as Krashen and others would have had us believe), young children acquiring their first language spend a great deal of their time producing or receiving playful language. They have, after all, only limited reasons to use language for practical purposes in a world in which their every move—what they wear, what they eat, where they go—is decided by somebody else . . . Thus, for young children a good deal of language remains primarily driven by sound rather than meaning, chosen to produce chance patterns which are pretty to the ear, but whose meaning may be absurd or unclear, as in this children's rhyme:

> Diddle diddle dumpling my son John
> Went to bed with his trousers on
> One shoe off and the other shoe on
> Diddle diddle dumpling my son John." (Cook 1997, p. 228)

When language hangs in what Cook calls "a friendly frame of sound," that is, rhymed rhythmic verse or the continuing sound of the adult voice reading to them, children are not troubled by words or expressions with no discernible referential meaning ("Diddle diddle dumpling . . ."). In subsequent conversation, children often by chance reveal amusing mis-hearings. For example, the words of the Lord's Prayer ("Lead us not into temptation") are misunderstood as "Lead us not into Penn Station" or the verse "Hallowed be thy name" is heard as "Howard be thy name" (Cook 1997, p. 229). Cook goes on to note that in contrast to this cavalier attitude toward meaning, child language is carefully focused on linguistic form. Many children's rhymes and stories emphasize grammatical patterns and appear to have much in common with so-called mechanical drills:

> This little piggy went to market,
> This little piggy stayed home,
> This little piggy had roast beef,
> This little piggy had none,
> and this little piggy cried
> "Wee, wee, wee," all the way home!

The undisputed centrality of the poetic function for child language does not necessarily mean that it has much import for adult second language learning. Adults, however, are fonder of language play than is generally acknowledged. Most scholars who have studied verbal art claim that the poetic function is found in both child and adult language—it never goes away (Friedrich 1986). The difference, then, is not the presence or absence of the poetic function but the degree to which it is present, as well as the relevant forms or genres of speech play (Kirshenblatt-Gimblett 1976).

One of the most prominent instances of language play is literature. Reading can be downright pleasurable no matter whether one prefers the classics or pulp fiction. In fact, fiction allows adults relief from the real world. Cook argues that "in literature, more than any other discourse, we see the fallacy of positing attention to form and to meaning as alternatives" (Cook 1997, p. 230). But language play and the poetic function are not only features of literary discourse. They are also quite evident in advertisements, jokes, newspaper headlines, graffiti—forms of discourse that are rife with puns, parallelisms, grammatical substitutions, and so on. In fact, as Tannen argues, even ordinary conversation is not as task-based and referential as proponents of CLT seem to believe. Conversational discourse is as much about the psychosocial as it is about the informational-cognitive.

Implications for Language Teaching

What implications might all this have for language teaching? I argue that the poetic function has been marginalized in foreign language methodology and should be restored by reinstating many discarded and reviled activities: explicit attention to form, manipulation of form, repetition, even rote learning. I am not proposing a return to the good old days of grammar translation and a belletristic curriculum. Nevertheless, I do see a role for many out-of-fashion activities.

Explicit Attention to Form

Language instruction has long been plagued by a continuing debate concerning the proper role of grammar instruction. Unfortunately, the debate has fostered a dichotomous approach to grammar instruction and a naive view of the nature of grammar. In the so-called traditional approach grammatical phenomena are assumed to be wholly amenable to explicit presentation and practice. In the other approach, teachers maintain that such linguistic analysis is largely irrelevant to acquisition. What is all-important is comprehensible input. Although these two approaches are opposites in many ways, they actually are both based on a conception of grammar that is monolithic: either grammar can be taught, or it cannot. Both conceptions of grammar are equally untenable (Blyth 1997).

The recent Focus-on-Form movement, the middle ground between these two extremes, is based on a more realistic conception of grammar as heterogeneous, that is, comprised of qualitatively different phenomena. Some grammatical points are axiomatic—easy to describe, easy to apply. Other items are essentially probabilistic statements about language use—difficult, if not impossible, to apply. Teachers intuitively understand that not all grammatical points are created equal, and yet there is still a widespread one-size-fits-all mentality (Doughty and Williams 1998).

Another fallacy fostered by the "great grammar debate" is the belief that grammar instruction is synonymous with explicit techniques. The real problem is that grammar instruction in both approaches is limited to a small set of pedagogical practices. In contrast, Focus-on-Form pedagogy profitably mixes explicit and implicit techniques depending on the grammatical item and the communicative task. In my mind, the greatest contribution of the

Focus-on-Form movement has been to demonstrate that there are many ways to focus on linguistic forms in the classroom. In other words, a form-focused activity need not be metalinguistic, as is typically the case; instead it may be poetic (in the Jakobsonian sense). The term *input enhancement,* Focus-on-Form jargon for the embedding of a given form in a text so that the reader pays more attention to the form, is nothing new. Skilled writers have been "enhancing the input" for millennia.

As a language program director looking for more creative ways to focus on linguistic form, I slowly reached the difficult conclusion that I would have to produce my own materials. My goal was to create a curriculum that mixed referential texts with texts that emphasized verbal artistry. As part of their apprenticeship in our program, teaching assistants are responsible for finding French texts that focus on the poetic function—songs, poetry, jokes, nursery rhymes. We are currently experimenting with various ways to use these poetic texts in class, sometimes as out-of-class readings, sometimes as choral readings in class, sometimes as the basis for game-like drills, sometimes as texts for listening comprehension.

Repetition, Rote Learning, Manipulation of Forms

In her article on repetition in conversational discourse, Tannen notes that negative attitudes toward repetition in language abound. For example, Tannen points out that the adjective *repetitious* in common usage is almost always pejorative. She cites W. H. Auden, who observed that repetition is associated in most people's minds with all that is most boring and lifeless, such as punching time clocks. Auden lamented that the denigration of repetition presents an obstacle for poetry, since this literary art form is based on the repetition of words and sounds in order to create aesthetic rhythms. Tannen blames the bad press of repetition on the conduit metaphor, according to which language is viewed as a neutral vehicle for conveying mostly referential information (Tannen 1987, p. 585).

Repetition in language teaching is usually associated with the greatly maligned mechanical drill. The technique of pattern practice rests on the assumption that short training sessions with a small number of exemplars, each of which is typically practiced once, will lead to fluency. Although most teachers no longer subscribe to such behavioristic notions of language learning, that does not mean that drills and repetition in general do not have a place in language classrooms. Furthermore, the jury is still out concerning the role of formulaic language in language learning. The anthropological linguist A. L. Becker has argued that grammar may be more a matter of the accumulation of prior texts that are remembered than the learning of abstract rules used in the generation of original utterances (Becker 1984). The linguist Dwight Bolinger argued for a similar account of linguistic competence:

> At present we have no way of telling the extent to which a sentence like *I went home* is a result of invention, and the extent to which it is a result of repetition, countless speakers before us having already said it and transmitted it to us *in toto*. Is grammar something where speakers produce constructions, or where they reach for them, from a preestablished inventory? (Bolinger 1961, p. 381)

Although the actual role of repetition in adult second language learning may still be unclear, there does seem to be a connection between what is spontaneously repeated by learners and linguistic or discursive form. Several years ago, my colleagues and I developed a CD-ROM to accompany the textbook we were using at the time (Blyth et al. 1995). The CD-ROM was developed with a research agenda in mind, and so we conducted several experiments concerning how students used multimedia for their own language learning. The CD-ROM consisted of approximately 170 screens, each with a text field, an image field, a notes field, and a set of comprehension questions. Vocabulary and grammatical points were annotated with hot links embedded in the texts. Thus, clicking on an underlined word would give the user various kinds of additional information—a translation, an image, and a brief grammatical or cultural explanation, if necessary. Students could also look up words in an on-line dictionary and record themselves in order to compare their accent to that of native speakers. The texts differed widely in both length and genre from very short informal dialogues to expository texts three to four paragraphs in length. A tracking device was programmed into the CD-ROM so that we could see exactly how students used the software. One conclusion that we gleaned from the tracking data was that students rarely recorded themselves. Of the 170 texts, only a handful seemed consistently to prompt students to record themselves. When I looked at the anomalous texts, I discovered that they were all highly structured and repetitive. For example, one text was titled "Quel temps fait-il aujourd'hui?" (What's the weather like today?). This text consisted entirely of weather expressions, which all belong to a grammatical frame:

Il fait beau.	*Il fait* du soleil.	*Il fait* du vent.
It is nice.	It is sunny.	It is windy.

Why did students spontaneously choose to repeat highly repetitive texts, instead of other, more conversational texts? Perhaps they were used to doing similar drill-like work in previous classrooms, and thus their behavior could have been an artifact of their experience with traditional language labs (Blyth 1999). Or it may be that students chose these texts because they were easy to imitate. In other words, the poetic structure of the texts made them similar to a pattern drill that lends itself to repetition since it requires only one new piece of information per sentence. Students quickly mastered the impersonal verb frame (Il fait . . .), thus allowing a level of automaticity not available with other texts. Rather than reject repetition as a throwback to outdated psychological theories, I think that we need to do much work in order to understand how repetition and imitation affect adult language learning and why.

Grammatical Exemplification

I have also recently endeavored to emphasize the poetic function in the production of an on-line pedagogical grammar for students of French at the University of Texas at Austin. The grammar Web site, called Tex's French Grammar, is designed to function as a reference grammar to be used in several different courses. Because reference grammars are typically not integrated with thematic vocabulary, these works are characterized by unrelated example sentences with little if any context. Since the lack of context frees language from its normal referential function, we decided to make that freedom into an advantage by emphasizing the poetic function. We followed the lead of the playwright Eugene Ionesco, who drew inspiration for his absurdist plays from the bizarre language found in pedagogical materials. A good example of the poetic function can be found in the dialogue exemplifying the word *tout* (all, every), which may function as an adjective, adverb, or pronoun in French. The main character, a Francophone armadillo named Tex, recites a love poem to impress his girlfriend.

Malgré *toutes* les filles	In spite of all the girls
que j'ai connues,	that I have known,
je pense à toi . . .	I think of you . . .
tout le temps,	all the time,
toute la journée,	all day long,
tous les soirs,	every evening,
toutes les nuits.	every night.

After reciting his poem, Tex is so pleased with himself that he exclaims:

Tout tatou est poète!	Every armadillo is a poet!

The poetic function is manifest in the repetition of the construction of the adjective *tout* followed by the definite article and the noun. It is also manifest in the repeated syllables of "Tout tatou est poète." The goal of these example sentences is to catch the fancy of our students, who seem to enjoy the whimsical nature of this reference grammar.

Recognition That the Language Classroom Is Not a Real World

And finally, reemphasizing the poetic function in our curriculum has helped us merge language practice with language play. Play can be loosely defined as behavior not primarily motivated by human need to manipulate the environment but rather to form and maintain social relationships. In contrast to Lee and VanPatten (1995), I find the language classroom ideally suited to the psychosocial uses of language and rather ill-suited at times to so-called real-world language tasks. After all, one of the hallmarks of play is that there are no consequences in the real world. Children can pretend to fight their mortal enemies on the battlefield, but once the game is over, wounds heal and the dead come back to life. Role-playing, for example, may be communicative in some respects but it is still essentially play. When the bell rings, students discard their roles and go on their way. In essence, the language classroom is a safe haven where language can be practiced without the fear of the negative consequences of linguistic errors in the real world.

Conclusion

In guise of conclusion, I summarize my major points as follows:

1. Many teachers who favor CLT hold questionable beliefs about the nature of communication. In general, proponents of CLT overemphasize the referential function and overlook the importance of the other functions, in particular the poetic.

2. Focusing on language form is neither as unnatural nor as inauthentic as many methodologists have recently argued. When linguistic forms are focused on in discourse, either the metalingual function or the poetic function is foregrounded.

3. The language classroom is well suited to language play. Purposeful language use should be profitably balanced with language play, the goal of which is to enjoy the aesthetic pleasure of linguistic creation.

4. Increasing the emphasis on the poetic function in the foreign language curriculum entails not only changes in method but also changes in content, that is, the reintroduction of literature and of songs so lacking in today's commercial textbooks.

I began this essay by juxtaposing two vastly different contexts of literacy: my French language classroom and my daughter's bedtime stories, including the masterpieces of children's literature by Dr. Seuss. In 1966 the columnist Ellen

Goodman wrote a review of this literary gem that is reprinted on the book's jacket: "Dr. Seuss took 220 words, rhymed them, and turned out *The Cat in the Hat,* a little volume of absurdity that worked like a karate chop on the weary little world of Dick, Jane, and Spot." It is my contention that the occasionally weary world of realia-based foreign language literacy would benefit from a similar karate chop of poetic language.

References

Becker, A. (1984). The Linguistics of Particularity. *Berkeley Linguistics Society* 10: 425–36.

Blyth, C. (1997). A Constructivist Approach to Grammar: Teaching Teachers to Teach Aspect. *Modern Language Journal* 81(1): 50–66.

———. (1999). Implementing Technology in the Foreign Language Curriculum: Redefining the Boundaries Between Language and Culture. *Educational Computing Research* 20(1): 39–58.

Blyth, C., K. Kelton, and E. Eubank. (1995). *Parallèles Interactive CD-ROM.* Upper Saddle River, N.J.: Prentice-Hall.

Bolinger, D. (1961). Syntactic Blends and Other Matters. *Language* 37: 366–81.

Caton, S. (1987). Contributions of Roman Jakobson. *Annual Review of Anthropology* 16: 223–60.

Cook, G. (1997). Language Play, Language Learning. *ELT Journal* 51(3): 224–31.

———. (2000). *Language Play, Language Learning.* Oxford: Oxford University Press.

Doughty, C., and J. Williams. (1998). *Focus on Form in Classroom Second Language Acquisition.* Cambridge: Cambridge University Press.

Friedrich, P. (1986). *The Language Parallax: Linguistic Relativism and Poetic Indeterminacy.* Austin: University of Texas Press.

Jakobson, R. (1960). Closing Statement: Linguistics and Poetics. In *Style in Language,* edited by T. A. Sebeok. Cambridge: MIT Press.

Kirshenblatt-Gimblett, B., ed. (1976). *Speech Play.* Philadelphia: University of Pennsylvania Press.

Kuczaj, S. (1983). *Crib Speech and Language Play.* New York: Springer-Verlag.

Lee, J. F., and B. VanPatten. (1995). *Making Communicative Language Teaching Happen.* New York: McGraw Hill.

Owens, R. (1996.) *Language Development: An Introduction.* Boston: Allyn and Bacon.

Tannen, D. (1987). Repetition in Conversation: A Poetics of Talk. *Language* 63(3): 574–605.

———. (1989). *Talking Voices: Repetition, Dialogue, and Imagery in Conversational Discourse.* Cambridge: Cambridge University Press.

VanLier, L. (1996). *Interaction in the Language Curriculum: Awareness, Autonomy, and Authenticity.* London: Longman.

Waugh, L. R., and M. Monville-Burston, eds. (1990). *On Language: Roman Jakobson.* Cambridge: Harvard University Press.

5

Reading Between the Cultural Lines

GILBERTE FURSTENBERG

Reading between the lines of any text is not a simple task. It requires an intimate knowledge of the writer's point of view, of his or her intent, and of the overall context, as well as a deep understanding of the subtleties of language. The meaning of a text or a sentence can therefore be constructed differently by different readers, depending on their level of awareness in any of these areas: one reader may interpret a text literally, whereas another may be able to see through its outward layers and gain access to its underlying meanings. Reading between the cultural lines—that is, seeing through the prism of another culture—is, of course, twice as difficult.

It is common for someone reading a text or listening to a story in a foreign language to construct culturally erroneous images, even if he or she understands the foreign language very well. A striking illustration of that phenomenon is to be found in Andreï Makine's book *Le Testament français* (*Dreams of Russian Summers*), which recounts the relationship between a little boy growing up in a town on the Russian steppes in the 1960s and his French-born grandmother, who, on her flower-covered balcony, often tells him stories from another time, another place: the Paris of her youth. Makine relates how he pictured in his mind what Neuilly, his French grandmother's birthplace, looked like as she recounted tales of her youth to him. He writes:

Our grandmother had said to us one day, when speaking of her birthplace, *"Oh! At that time Neuilly was just a village . . ."* She had said it in French, but we only knew Russian villages. And a village in Russia is inevitably a ring of *izbas;* indeed the very word in Russian, *derevnya,* comes from *derevo*—a tree, wood. The confusion persisted, despite the clarifications that Charlotte's stories would later bring. At the name, *"Neuilly,"* we had immediate visions of the village, with its wooden houses, its herd and its cockerel. And when, the following summer, Charlotte spoke to us for the first time about a certain Marcel Proust—*"by the way, we used to see him playing tennis at Neuilly, on the Boulevard Bineau"*—we pictured the dandy with big languorous eyes (she had shown us his photo) there among the *izbas!*

Beneath the patina of our French words Russian reality often showed through. The president of the Republic was bound to have something Stalinesque about him in the portrait sketched by our imagination. *Neuilly* was peopled with *kolkhozniks.* (Makine 1997, pp. 23–24)

Reading between the cultural lines is indeed difficult, because it requires a double kind of translation: first a literal translation of the text and then the ability to transpose oneself and one's imagination into the author's or speaker's foreign world. It is a difficult skill to acquire, yet an essential one, for the purpose of developing true literacy in a foreign language. It requires accessing, seeing, reaching the imbedded layers of emotions, judgments, and implicit connotations lurking behind a foreign reality and a foreign text, whether a literary piece, a news article, a story, or even an administrative document.

The question, of course, is this: How can we help our students achieve this level of understanding? I shall not pretend that I have all the answers or that I have found the only and definitive way. What I want to do is present one way in which that kind of reading—reading through the cultural lines—can be made easier and more achievable than ever before through an innovative use of technology, in this case of the Web and its network-based communication tools.

What I shall briefly describe is a Web-based project that my colleagues Shoggy Waryn (formerly of MIT and now at Brown University) and Sabine Levet (formerly of MIT and now at Brandeis University) and I developed at MIT over a period of four years: a project designed to develop students' in-depth understanding of another culture. *Cultura,* as it is called, is a large-scale project funded by the National Endowment for the Humanities and the Consortium for Language Teaching and Learning. I shall not describe *Cultura* in great detail; a more specific account of the project is to be found at the project Web site ⟨http://llt.msu.edu/vol5num1/furstenberg/default.html⟩. It is not my purpose here, especially considering that the primary goal of *Cultura* is not to develop reading comprehension per se but rather to develop cross-cultural understanding. Reading, and in particular cross-cultural reading, however, are part and parcel of the project. Not only does the written word form its central component, but there are also many parallels to be drawn between the reading of a culture and the reading of a text. It is on this particular junction that I wish to focus this chapter.

Understanding another culture is, as we know, a difficult and life-long process—especially when we talk about understanding foreign attitudes, values, beliefs, and ways of interacting with and looking at the world. These notions are also very difficult to teach, because they are essentially elusive, abstract, invisible. The question then becomes: How does one make something that is essentially invisible visible, something that is essentially inaccessible accessible?

An approach that has worked well is one that is built on a comparative approach based on the process of juxtaposition. What *Cultura* offers is a comparative, cross-cultural approach whereby American students taking an intermediate French class at MIT and French students taking an English class at the Institut National des Télécommunications in Evry, France, working together for the duration of a whole semester analyze together a variety of similar materials that originate from both countries and are presented in juxtaposition on the Web. These materials are organized according to modules that range from questionnaires to opinion polls, films, news media, and texts. Then students exchange in writing, through open on-line forums, their viewpoints and perspectives on the subjects at hand. Through these cross-cultural exchanges (written in their own native language) students share observations, send queries, and answer their counterparts' questions, with the goal of better understanding the other's viewpoints and deepening their understanding of foreign perspectives.

To support the claim that such cross-cultural encounters can indeed be powerful allies in the understanding of a foreign culture (and—within it—of a foreign text), I would like to cite the Russian critic Mikhail Bakhtin, who wrote, "A meaning only reveals its depths once it has encountered and come into contact with another foreign meaning" (Bakhtin 1986, p. 7). For the purpose of this essay, I shall focus on what I consider to be the central word here—*meaning*—because unearthing the meaning of a foreign word, a foreign text, or a foreign point of view is indeed the central element that will allow a student to "read" fully and truly between the cultural lines.

Such a goal cannot be realized in any single moment. It is the result of a process. And this is what *Cultura* is all about: taking students along a process that will help them gradually build the skills that will better enable them to read, literally and figuratively, a foreign culture. This reading is done in a series of stages, which I shall now illustrate, in which the reading of a text, the unearthing of hidden connotations and meanings, play a major part.

In the first stage, students on both sides of the Atlantic answer, in their native language, a series of three questionnaires (the English and French questionnaires are mirror images of each other). They include the following:

- a word-association questionnaire that asks students to say what words they associate with such words as *success* or *réussite; freedom* or *liberté; authority* or *autorité; individualism* or *individualisme; suburb* or *banlieue*, and so on;
- a sentence-completion questionnaire, in which students finish such sentences as "a good neighbor is someone who . . ." or "*un bon voisin est quelqu'un qui . . .*"; "a good citizen" or "*un bon citoyen*"; and "a good parent" or "*un bon parent*"; and
- a situation-reaction questionnaire, in which students spontaneously react to such situations as the following: "you see a mother in a supermarket slap her child" or "*vous voyez une mère dans un supermarché qui gifle son enfant.*"

Note that students answer these questionnaires in their own "native" language or, rather, in the language of the country in which they are studying (not all MIT students taking the French class are American). The fact that students write in their own language has three advantages:

1. There is no linguistic dominance, so students in the United States and in France are on an equal footing. This linguistic parity goes a long way in creating a sense of community.

2. Students are able to express and develop their thoughts fully in their native language.

3. The language and discourse that students experience are totally authentic.

After students have responded, the answers are posted on the Web in a juxtaposed fashion, as shown in table 5.1 (from the fall semester of 2000), with the words *suburb* and *banlieu*. (For the sake of authenticity, we decided not to eliminate spelling or typographical errors, unless they rendered the words or sentence incomprehensible. We did not add missing accents, either.)

The juxtaposition of these two words (each of which is the only possible translation of the other) clearly highlights how impossible it is to interchange

*Table 5.1 American and French Students' Response to the Topic "Suburb"
or "Banlieu"*

Suburb	Banlieu
· automobiles, dogs, picket fences	· adaptation
· boring, grid, cars	· alentours, quartiers
· boring, hills	· chic, insécurité, misère
· calm, quiet, peaceful	· Clichés, Préjugés
· cozy	· defavorisés, aide
· grass, dogs	· delinquence, innovation
· green, farm, peaceful	· Dependance
· Home, family	· déclin, insécurité ghettos, problème
· home, family	de société
· houses, cars, commuting	· défavorisée, pauvre
· houses, families, quiet	· entassement, sans vie, béton
· houses, flats, quiet	· Hétéroclite Paisible Peu sécurisante
· houses, lawns, middle class	· intégration, violence
· houses, trees, fields	· maison, exageration
· jersey, town	· misère, violence
· Middle Class, Complicated,	· non-droit, violence, avenir
Lonely	· porfois agréable
· my town, NYC, awesome	· pauvre, pavillon, ennui
· new york city, middle class	· pauvreté, délinquance
· nice, home, quiet	· problèmes, délinquance
· quiet silence dull	· problèmes, cités, délinquance
· quiet, nice, boring, malls	· problèmes, embouteillages, cité
· quiet, peaceful, outskirts	· RER, rap
· silence, boredom	· tag, pit bull, drogue, raket,
· sparse, trees	immigrés
· suburbia	· toujours à découvrir
· trees, mini-vans	· transports, urbanisme
· wealth, growth	· trouble, fruit des erreurs du passé
	(60s)
· white, rich, safe	· violence, guettos, drogues
· white, wealthy, sheltered	· violence, oubliées, emmigrés

their realities. In the same way as Neuilly is no Russian village, Pantin, a
banlieue of Paris, is no Lexington, Massachusetts. Immediately, a small window opens on the opposite socioeconomic realities of a French *banlieue* and
an American suburb. Even though France now has *banlieues résidentielles,*
which are more akin to the American model, the typical French *banlieue,*

with its *criminalité, ghettos, délinquance, violence,* and *danger,* is much more akin to the American inner city.

The same process of juxtaposition allows striking differences in concepts to emerge clearly as well, as is evident in the responses to the words *individualism* and *individualisme* from the fall 2000 experiment, shown in table 5.2. The sheer juxtaposition of these words brings to light the deeper meanings

Table 5.2 American and French Students' Response to the Topic "Individualism"

Individualism	Individualisme
• cities, US, style	• arrivisme
• creativity self-containment alienation	• capacité, challenge, exclusion
• creativity, uniqueness	• danger
• essential, growth, potential	• danger, orgeuil
• Europe, Self-Knowing	• difficile, irrealiste
• express, freedom, distinquished	• echec, c'est fini
• express, unique, different	• egoisme, personnel, protection
• expression, unique	• Egoïsme, Etats-unis
• free speech, pot	• exacerbé, liberté, démocratie
• free speech, eccentricity	moderne
• free, be your own person	• Force de caractèce, Isolationisme
• freedom, narrowminded, capitalism	• égocentrisme, égoïsme
• freedom, one person	• égoïsme, haine
• freedom, power	• égoïsme, lutte, asocial
• frontier, civil liberties	• égoïsme, solitaire
• important, free	• indépendance
• Independance, selfishness, courage	• inutile
• independent, unique	• isolement
• liberty, free-thinking, confidence	• moi, ma philosophie indispensable
• personality, awareness	• néfaste, collectif
• point of view, Kafka, Existentialism	• négatif, égoisme
• positive, cool, ethical	• néfaste, groupe
• security, unique	• personnalité, égoisme, carisme
• self-sufficiency, careerism, self-	• positif, modernité, valorisant
development	• repli sur soi, absence d'échange
• strength, creativity, loneliness	• Solitude, Archarnement
uncommon	• solitude, laissé pour compte, égoisme
• unique, different, important	• vie, propriété caractère
• uniqueness, individual	• égoïsme, solitude
• USA, selfishness	

this word and this concept have for an American and a French person. Whereas highly positive connotations such as freedom, creativity, and personal expression constantly appear on the American side, the French side is replete with such negative notions as *égoïsme, égocentrisme,* and *solitude.*

This side-by-side presentation of the two words helps students immediately access the underlying value of the word and realize that what may be viewed as a very positive notion and presented in a very positive light in one culture may not be viewed or understood as such by the reader or interlocutor of another culture.

Not all words or sentences or situations yield such obviously differing views. Most require a much closer reading but will reveal, on closer examination, interesting observations. Let us look, for instance, at the fall 2000 responses to *A well-behaved child* and *Un enfant bien élevé* (table 5.3). Readers

Table 5.3 American and French Students' Responses Concerning Children

A Well-Behaved Child	Un Enfant Bien Élevé
· listens to their parents	· d'autonome
· polite, attentive	· d'heureux
· polite, deferential, respectful	· d'honnête, qui ne doit pas mentir sauf
· that listens to their parents	pour une bonne cause
· who acts well in public	· de sage
· who behaves in public and doesn't	· est poli, qui sait bien se tenir
make a scene	· qui est équilibré psychiquement et
· who can be respectful in a public	physiquement
place	· obéit, qui sais se comporter
· who can control his temper	· qui a reçu une bonne éducation
· who knows what authority is, who a	· qui aide au tâches ménagères, se tiend
stranger can take care of and still feel	bien à table, est serviable et poli
in charge	· qui dit merci et s'il vous plait et qui se
· who does not cry in public	tient bien à table
· who does not need a spanking in the	· qui dit bonjour à la dame
supermarket	· qui dit bonjour sans qu'on lui
· who doesn't cry or throw tantrums	demande de le faire
but explains what they want	· qui est intéressé et attentif
· who doesn't interrupt people who are	· qui est poli, gentil
talking	· qui est respectueux envers les
· who is himself/herself . . . but listens	personnes plus âgées que lui
to others	· qui ferme sa bouche quand il mange
· who is not rude	· qui n'est pas égoiste
· who is quiet and polite	· qui n'impose pas sa volonté aux autres
· who is respectful, caring, and sincere	

Table 5.3   Continued

A Well-Behaved Child	Un Enfant Bien Élevé
• who knows his place • who knows what is permitted and what not; that child won't insist on his parents buying him a new toy once they have told him 'no' • who knows when it is OK to act up and when not • who learns that something is right or wrong when taught • who listens to his parents • who listens to his parents • who listens to his parents • who listens to its mother • who listens to their parents and other authority figures • who obeys his parents, who does not yell • who respects others • who respects others. • with good parents	• qui pense par lui meme • qui repecte ses camarades et les adultes qu'il rencontre • qui respecte ceux qui l'entourent • qui respecte les autres et écoute les adultes • qui respecte les autres, est poli • qui respecte son entourage, se respecte lui-meme, écoute les plus vieux • qui respecte tout le monde, comme les inconnus • qui sait se montrer discret quand sa présence est malvenue • qui sait se tenir chez les autres • qui se tient bien à table, qui a appris à avoir un sens critique aiguisé, qui est bien dans sa peau • qui saura sadapter partout et qui sera apprécié des autres parents. • qui est capable d'agir de maniére autonome en sinserant dans la sociiété à une place qu'il aura librement choisie. • qui respecte tout le monde, ses parents comme les inconnus • qui sait se montrer discret quand sa présence est malvenue • qui sait se tenir chez les autres • qui se tient bien à table, qui a appris à avoir un sens critique aiguisé, qui est bien dans sa peau • qui saura s'adapter partout et qui sera apprécié des autres parents. • qui est capable d'agir de maniére autonome en s'inserant dans la société à une place qu'il aura librement choisie.

who know French will probably remark that these sentences are not an equal translation of each other. Indeed, the literal translation of *un enfant bien élevé* would be "a well-brought-up child"; *une personne impolie* would be translated by "an impolite person." We (the French and American instructors at MIT and INT) have deliberately chosen expressions that are commonly used in both languages. An initial examination of the responses about a well-behaved child and *un enfant bien élevé* reveals, among other things, one very interesting difference: the emphasis, on the American side, on the relationship between the child and his or her parents and, on the French side, on the relationship between a child and *les autres* (other people), the latter being everyone else but the parents. As can be seen from the responses above, the only times the word *parent* is mentioned on the French side are in the following two examples:

> qui respecte tout le monde, ses parents comme des inconnus (who respects everyone, his or her parents as well as strangers) [Here the parents are just one group among others]

> qui saura s'adapter partout et qui sera apprécié des *autres* [my emphasis] parents (who knows how to adjust everywhere and who are appreciated by other parents)

In other words, a well-behaved child, *à la française,* is a child who has learned his or her lessons well at home and can apply them outside the home, with people other than his or her parents.

A subsequent close look at what constitutes a rude person or *une personne impolie* reveals that politeness on the French side is clearly of a social nature. A *personne impolie* is someone who *"a oublié son savoir-vivre chez soi"* (forgot his or her manners at home), *"qui ne dit pas 'merci, s'il vous plaît,'" "qui ne respecte pas les bonnes manières"* (who does not say "thank you," "please," who does not use good manners). On the American side, by contrast, politeness has a much more affective slant. Indeed, a rude person in the American style is someone who is not considerate of other people, does not care about other people's feelings, does not respect the feelings of others, or is insensitive to other people's feelings. Whereas the word *respect* appears frequently on both sides, it is also clear that what the French tend to respect are good manners and social behaviors, whereas the focus of the Americans' respect is the person, and in particular the person's feelings, as will be obvious from table 5.4.

The prevalence of words such as *to care, inconsiderate, feelings* readily leads students to wonder what the equivalent of such words might be in French. As it turns out, there is no equivalent. There is no way of translating phrases such as "How do you feel?" The direct translation in French would be "Comment tu te sens?," which in French refers only to the physical well-being of a

Table 5.4 American and French Students' Responses Concerning Rudeness

A Rude Person	Une Personne Impolie
• annoying, over-bearing • interrupts and not listen • isn't considerate of other people. • shows people no respect • that says inconsiderate things • who cuts you in line. • who disregards the people around him/her. • who disrespects opinions which differ from his own, who knows the unwritten rules of conduct and chooses to break them anyway. • who does not respect others • who doesn't care about other peoples' feelings • who doesn't care about others. • who doesn't listen to others before expressing an opinion, who disrespects others • who doesn't respect the rights or feelings of others • who doesn't take others into consideration • who ignores others • who insults others and is not considerate of others feelings • who is a poor winner • who is disrespectful • who is ignorant • who is inconsiderate of other people's feelings • who is inconsiderate to others • who is insensitive to others' feelings • who is not respectful • who is obnoxious • who is selfish, greedy, and thoughtless • who openly attacks unjustifiably • who oversteps his or her bounds • who pushes people in a crowd to get to the front	• à qui je préfère ne pas adresser la parole • d'ininteressant, de faible • de bestial, qui ne s'integre pas bien dans la société, qui se fout des conventions établies • de traumatisée • qui a oublié son savoir-vivre chez soi • qui a une tenue incorrect vis-à-vis d'autrui, qui bouscule une personne âgée • qui est grossier, rustre et irrespectueux • qui est vulgaire, qui est grossiere • qui n'éprouve aucune gêne envers les autres dans ses actes et paroles • qui ne dit pas "merci," "s'il vous plaît" • qui ne tient pas la porte, qui rentre dans l'ascenseur avant que les autres sortent, etc • qui ne dit pas bonjour • qui ne fait jamais l'effort de penser avec les yeux d'autrui • qui ne respecte pas l'autre • qui ne respecte pas les autres ni les usages de la vie en société • qui ne respecte pas les bonnes manières ou qui ne fait pas attention aux autres • qui ne respecte pas les usages • qui ne respecte pas son prochain • qui ne respecte que "son nombril" • qui ne se respecte pas, ne respecte pas son interlocuteur, qui refuse de comprendre et d'intégrer les coutumes de son interlocuteur • qui ne se retient jamais • qui ne se soucie pas des attentes des autres • qui ne vous respecte pas

Table 5.4 Continued

A Rude Person	Une Personne Impolie
• who talks when other people are talking	• qui pense tout d'abord à elle-même, et qui n'hésitera pas à s'inviter chez des gens qu'elle connaît • qui répond mal et qui se mouche dans les rideaux • qui sénerve quand il n'est pas d'accord • qui se fiche des autres • qui vous bouscule sans s'excuser • qui vous marche sur les pieds sans dire pardon • sans respect

person (for example, "je me sens bien" or "je me sens mal"). Similarly, there is no way of translating "I understand your feelings" or "she is a very caring, considerate person." The closest would be "Je comprends ce que tu veux dire" ("I understand what you *mean*").

Again, the simple process of juxtaposition makes the readers aware of the connotations and meanings of words as well as the impossibility of always transposing one word with another in another culture. It allows students to reach a real sense of the interconnectedness of language and culture. To echo Bahktin's words, "A meaning only reveals its depths once it has encountered and come into contact with another foreign meaning."

In the next step of *Cultura,* students are encouraged to look for patterns and to see whether the observations they made in one specific context can be transferred to other contexts. By making cross-analyses—links between different words, sentences, or situations—students will notice, for instance, that American students tend frequently to inject an affective slant into many situations, whereas French students tend to look at a situation from a much more rational or even aloof point of view. For instance, when answering questions about *un bon parent, un bon prof, un bon médecin* (a good parent, a good teacher, a good doctor), the French tend to give responses pertaining to the role or function of that person. *Un bon médecin* and *un bon prof* are, above all, professionally competent, and in France a good parent is someone who *éduque* his or her children in the French sense of the word, that is, instills values. Americans, on the other hand, often seem to place, again, a much higher value on affective qualities. A good parent loves unconditionally; a good doctor is caring; a good teacher is someone who can teach *and* care, or who deeply cares about the learning process.

Each word, sentence, situation offered to the students for analysis then leads to a forum, which in turn provides yet another crucial resource for helping them read between the cultural lines. These Web-based forums, written in the students' native language, are central to the task, because they provide students with the opportunity to enter into an exchange with their counterparts, to ask for help in deciphering meanings of words or concepts, to present their own hypotheses and points of view, and to ask for help in verifying these hypotheses. The forums provide a common space for negotiating meanings and interpretations, as is shown in the examples below.

Example 1 (from the fall 2000 forums) illustrates the type of questions a French student will ask and the type of response an American student will give concerning the words United States/*Etats-Unis*. Again, student input is unedited.

> A. R. (INT)—10:33am Oct 9, 2000 (#2 of 49)
>
> Dans ce questionnaire vous insistez sur 'opportunity', mais dans quel sens: de rencontrer de nombreuses personnes, de faire des expériences variées, de travail? (In this questionnaire, you insist on "opportunity" but in what sense? in the sense of meeting many people? having varied work experiences?)

To this two American students responded as follows:

> S. T. (MIT)—02:12am Oct 15, 2000 (#12 of 49)
>
> By opportunity, we mean it in many different ways. For example, the people of America are very diverse, and especially in college, we make friends that come from all different backgrounds (cultural, economic, etc). The opportunities to study whatever we want is very apparent, since in most universities, you have until sophomore year to declare a major. From talking to several French friends this summer, I got the sense that they were never exposed to lots of other cultures that I have been exposed to (Korean, even Vietnamese, whose country was taken over by France several decades ago), and one of them told me he had to narrow down his choice of major ever since high school and has never taken courses outside of his major. Also, I believe jobs are easier to find.

> P. T. (MIT)—06:25pm Oct 15, 2000 (#18 of 49)
>
> Hello Alex,
> Let my try to answer your question regarding the word "opportunity." Opportunity is basically used in the sense of work, in the sense of going up in the hierarchical pyramid of society. Work opportunities in this country are

greater than in most other countries. The rate at which people changes jobs is much greater than that of Europe. Unemployment is also much lower. This can lead to better lifestyles, etc. etc.

Certainly, such clarifications of the word provide a richer explanation than the one found in any dictionary. They also have the advantage of providing a totally contextualized insider's view of a word and a sense of its different shades of meaning.

In example 2 (from the fall 2000 forum the words freedom and *liberté*) it is shown how an association of words commonly made in one culture may be perceived as problematic by another.

V. G. (int-evry.fr)—10:02am Oct 9, 2000 (#1 of 23)

Pourquoi associer liberté et religion? (Why associate freedom and religion?)

Two replies to the French student who asked this question are given below.

R. S.—05:38pm Oct 15, 2000 (#10 of 23)

Vincent,
Liberty is associated with freedom of religion. This is especially so in the US where the constitution guarantees the right to believe in and practise different religions. So one has the freedom or liberty to choose one's own religion and practise it as she thinks fit.

In answer 2, another American student builds on the same point.

E. W.—08:51am Oct 16, 2000 (#13 of 23)

America was founded by people who wanted to escape religious persecution. Because of this, freedom of religion was incorporated in the Constitution as a fundamental right of American citizens. Now, freedom of religion and the freedom of thought is an integral part of American society. In my opinion, this is why Americans link liberty and religion.

Such forums provide an apt means of illuminating the historical roots of a phenomenon, and in this case, for explaining to the French the reasons why the words *freedom* and *religion* are so closely associated.

A detailed look at another forum demonstrates how American and French students tried to elucidate for each other their different concepts of *individualisme* and to build, with each other's help, a better understanding of what this word represents in their respective cultures. In the process of doing so, students made observations, drew hypotheses, responded to issues raised, and raised issues themselves, getting an increasingly closer look into each other's culture. The example below is taken from the forums of fall 1999 (for a look at the whole transcript, see the appendix to this chapter).

The forum started in the following manner. A French student began by summarizing the obvious differences he has seen emerge out of the juxtaposition of the words *individualism* and *individualisme*. He writes, "Visiblement [What an appropriate way to begin!], notre conception du mot individualism ou individualisme n'est pas du tout la même! En effet en France, celui-ci a un sens plutôt péjoratif très associé au sens du mot égoisme. Pour vous, il semble plutôt que ce soit la considération naturelle envers un individu, un mot associé au sens de liberté individuelle. En France, on est plus enclin à s'intéresser au groupe et l'individu a moins de place" (Obviously, our notion of the word *individualism* or *individualisme* is completely different! Indeed in France that word has a rather pejorative meaning closely associated with the word *egotism*. For you, it seems it has more to do with a natural consideration toward an individual, a word associated with the notion of individual freedom. In France, we are more inclined to be interested in the group, and the individual plays less of a role).

Another French student, Karine, made a similar summary and ended by wondering whether, though she finds the *esprit d'initiative* (entrepreneurial spirit) a very good thing, it might not get in the way of teamwork. Her phrasing made it clear that, in her mind, the two are incompatible. "Ainsi, pour les américains, l'esprit d'initiative est très valorisé et je trouve cela très bien, mais ne pensez-vous pas que le travail de groupe est aussi très enrichissant?" (So, for Americans, the entrepreneurial spirit is highly valued and I think that is good. But don't you think that group work is also very fulfilling?) Such remarks reinforce the American students' initial perceptions that the French seem to value *le groupe* much more than *l'individu*.

A French student, Anne-Laure, then intervened with a hypothesis as to the reasons behind the American emphasis on the "self": "Peut-être cette différence est-elle due à l'histoire des Etats-Unis, nation plus récente, où les autodidactes sont encouragés, tout comme l'esprit d'initiative, dans la création d'entreprises ou en recherche par exemple" (This difference may be due to the history of the United States, a more recent nation where self-made men as well as the entrepreneurial spirit were encouraged in order to create businesses or research, for example).

Michael, yet another French student, then wondered if this whole issue might not just be a matter of semantics: "C'est sans doute plus un problème de vocabulaire que de culture, car je ne crois pas que 'l'égoïsme,' ou la 'fermeture d'esprit' (associations que font les Français) soient des qualités aux Etats-Unis. L'individualisme au sens américain du terme se rapprocherait plutôt de ce que nous appelons le 'développement personnel' ou l'affirmation de soi." (This is probably more a semantic issue than a cultural one, because I don't think that "egotism" or "closedness of mind" [the associations made by the French] are viewed as qualities in the United States. Individualism in the American sense would be closer to what we call personal development or self-assertion.)

At this point, the first American student, Catherine, expressed her total shock at such opposing French and American points of view and wrote: "Hi everyone! When I first read the words all of you used associating to 'individualism,' I felt completely shocked. The ideal that Americans hold so closely to themselves is scorned by another country! It is so fascinating that we have such different interpretations of the 'same' word!" Then, responding to a point raised earlier by one of the French students, she went on: "An egotist is also looked badly upon here. 'Individualism' in our terms means independence. The connotation concentrates on the idea that a person does not need to and should not conform to all the ideas other people have. Everyone should think for himself or herself. It is important to us not to have to depend on others for everything." She responded to yet another point raised by the French by making clear that there is no incompatibility whatsoever between the notion of individualism and teamwork: "A few of you mentioned the idea of group work as well. We believe that group work is a good thing. An egotist would not participate in a group because he/she would think that he/she is too good and smart for the group. Yet an individual would work in a group because he/she can share their individually thought up ideas with the group to result in more ideas generated."

Finally, Catherine attempted to hypothesize why there might be such differences between the French and the American views: "But I do think that it has a lot to do with the way the U.S. developed into a country. When the colonies were under British rules, most of the normal people did as they were told. But a few individuals realized that people deserved better so they got together and shared their ideas and ideals. That eventually led to a revolution and the rest is history. Perhaps at one time, those few individuals were seen as egotists trying to do something completely crazy. Maybe because they succeeded, the term individualism slowly developed in a more positive light. Or maybe I am completely wrong with that idea."

Matthew, another American student, intervened and, building on Catherine's attempt at an explanation wrote: "As she [Catherine] mentioned, the United States grew out of a desire to be independent from Britain whereas France grew out of a desire for equality for all. The French revolution resulted in the removal of nobles with an unequal share of rights and privileges. Americans view individualism as growing above your environment to be the most you can."

Then Miranda came in, responding directly to Karine's question about whether individualism might get in the way of teamwork. She wrote: "In response to Karine, I think that the United States does praise individualism, however, not at the expense of teamwork. Especially in education, teamwork is considered vital to learning. I don't think that the two have to be considered opposing ideas."

Claudiu, another MIT student, concurred: "To answer Karine: Working in groups is definitely a good thing. I'm thinking of study groups, for example, which are quite popular at MIT (although not allowed by some courses). When solving a problem of general interest say for a company working in a group is a requirement. However, shaping one's own career (to illustrate the positive connotation of individualism) cannot be a group activity."

At this point, the French students presumably were aware that their initial premise about the incompatibility of individualism with teamwork was a faulty one. Through the comments from the MIT students, they were also given a glimpse of education at the Institute.

The discussion took a new turn when Christian, a French student, made another type of distinction: he noticed that the French reactions to the word *individualisme* tended to be negative when put in a personal context but more positive when seen within an institutional context. He wrote: "Ainsi, du côté des réponses positives, les français décrivent l'individualisme d'un point de vue 'institutionnel' (capitalisme, libéralisme, indépendance, liberté), tandis que les Américains se situent dans une logique plus 'personnelle.' L'individualisme n'est dès lors pas un comportement propre à un ensemble social ou le fruit d'une doctrine, mais le fruit d'une décision personnelle, justement en rupture avec la société, comme en témoignent les réponses mode de vie, anticonformisme, choix. En revanche, lorsqu'il s'agit des aspects négatifs les français se situent au niveau strictement individuel. L'individualiste devient alors un être égocentrique, solitaire et fermé d'esprit." (So, if one looks at the positive responses, the French describe individualism from an institutional point of view [capitalism, liberalism, independence, freedom] whereas the Americans situate themselves within a more personal framework. As a consequence, individualism [for the Americans] is not the behavior of a social group or the result of a doctrine but the result of a personal decision, precisely in opposition to society, as is shown by such examples as "way of life," "nonconformist," "choice." On the other hand, when talking about the negative aspects, the French situate themselves strictly at an individual level. An individualist then becomes egocentric, solitary and closed-minded.)

Then Ludovic offered a compromise view, although his fear of individualism showed through: "Il y a, je pense, à prendre des deux côtés: nous aurions à gagner en France à laisser développer l'imagination, la créativité des individus; mais il y a, aux US, un 'revers de médaillon': à trop vouloir pousser l'individualisme, il me semble qu'on s'isole toujours un peu plus." (There is, I believe, something to be learned from both sides: it would be to our advantage in France to nurture the imagination and creativity of individuals; but there is also the other side of the coin in the United States: if one pushes the notion of individualism too far, it seems that one might get more and more isolated.)

Finally, Liana, an MIT student, presented yet another perspective by adding a word of caution to the French: do not think that individualism is looked on positively by everybody. It may be the case at MIT, but "I think that among some other groups in America, individualism is not seen so positively. There are many stories of people who have different opinions, different fashions, etc. being considered wrong or dangerous by their communities (schools, towns, and so on). So I don't think that every American would agree that individualism is a good characteristic, even though it is very important to me."

Such conversations go a long way in making students better attuned to each other's differing cultural perspectives and in bridging their initial cultural gap.

In terms of language per se, these forums provide our students with an extraordinary source of authentic French language, in terms of vocabulary and discourse. The MIT students regularly bring back into the classroom French comments they have found particularly illuminating and relate them to their classmates via words they have "borrowed" from the French. By virtue of being written in the students' "native" language, the forums also offer—for the Americans—living examples of authentic French discourse, which then becomes an object of analysis in its own right. Quite often MIT students will notice how the French tend almost systematically to present both sides of the coin: the word *mais* (but) appears repeatedly. They will also remark on how highly structured the French discourse is ("Ainsi, du côté des réponses positives, les Français . . . tandis que les Américains . . ." "L'individualisme n'est dès lors pas . . . mais le fruit d'une décision personnelle, justement en rupture avec la société, comme en témoignent les réponses. . . . En revanche, lorsqu'il s'agit des aspects négatifs. . . . L'individualiste devient alors un être égocentrique."

Interestingly enough, students almost always spontaneously model the French discourse in their own subsequent writings in French. It is important at this point to emphasize that the MIT students use English *only* on the Web. The class discussions and the writings are always done in French. The reverse is true for the INT students.

Now in normal educational circumstances, students do not have an informant at their side assisting them in deciphering the hidden meanings of a text; they need to be able to do that on their own. *Cultura* constitutes a stepping stone, helping students become more fully aware of embedded cultural assumptions and better equipped for decoding a foreign meaning. The questionnaires and their accompanying forums, however, constitute only the first stage. Students then compare many other materials, such as French and American national opinion polls (so as to put their earlier findings into a much broader and more objective sociocultural framework), a French film and its American remake, news as portrayed in the American and the French press, and a variety of historical, literary, and sociological texts. Each time, students are expected to transfer their newly found cross-cultural skills to the reading of these texts and contexts.

Students will, for instance, work with the printed news and compare not only what the *New York Times* and *Le Monde* cover on a given day but how they cover the same event. One day, two students, completely on their own initiative, did a comparative study of the way both newspapers talked about Chechnya. Not only did they describe what events the newspapers focused on, but they analyzed the contexts that the newspapers supplied, or did not supply, and even the words used when referring to Russia and Chechnya. They came up with extraordinary insights that clearly brought out the respective underlying points of view. I am convinced that, had they not worked with *Cultura* before then, their level of analysis would have been much less subtle and sophisticated.

Toward the end of the semester, students are clearly able to access the underlying and implicit judgments found in a French text. For instance, when reading an article from the French newsmagazine *Le Point* (17 October 1998) titled *"Les nouveaux pionniers francais,"* which describes life for the French pioneers in Silicon Valley, students never fail to uncover the underlying biases contained in the introduction to the article:

> Diplômes français en poche, ils sont déjà 40.000 à avoir débarqué dans la "Valley," véritable locomotive des hautes technologies et des nouveaux médias. Pour ces émigrés de luxe, un eldorado, mais au prix de conditions de vie pas spécialement gaies.

(With French diplomas in their pockets, 40,000 of them have already disembarked in the Valley, that real locomotive of high technology and new media. For these deluxe immigrants, an Eldorado but with a particularly unfortunate toll on lifestyle.)

Our students are able to see it all: "Diplômes français en poche" (the pride of the French to see that their degrees are really prized in the United States!); "ils débarquent" (the mythical voyage!); "ces émigrés de luxe, un eldorado" (Ah, the call of money! That's what the United States is all about!); and the inevitable *mais,* followed by "au prix de conditions de vie pas spécialement gaies" (implicit message: life in France is much better). By that point in the course, our students could almost have taken on the persona of a French journalist and written that article.

My colleagues and I are often surprised to discover how deep and insightful some of the students' comments are and how proficient they become at identifying cultural features and at making relevant connections—to the point where their perceptions, unbeknownst to them, match the findings of cross-cultural experts.

In that context, it is worth revisiting Matthew's words in the forum about "individualism": "The United States grew out of a desire to be independent from Britain whereas France grew out of a desire for equality for all. The French revolution resulted in the removal of nobles with an unequal share of rights and privileges." He was unknowingly echoing the words of Tocqueville, who had written in 1830: "Le grand avantage des Américains est d'être arrivés à la démocratie sans avoir à souffrir des révolutions démocratiques et d'être nés égaux avant de le devenir" (De Toqueville 1961, p. 147). (The great advantage of the Americans is that they have reached freedom without having had to suffer through democratic revolutions and to have been born equal as opposed to becoming equal.)

This excerpt is one of those provided to the students in the library module, the final one in the *Cultura* process. Such texts, by virtue of being accessed at the end, instead of at the beginning, take on a lot more resonance for the students. They help the *Cultura* students measure how far they have come in the process of deciphering French culture and discover how close their own analysis sometimes comes to that of these experts. These texts also help illuminate the historical and philosophical roots of cultural phenomena that they themselves have deduced. The excerpt by Tocqueville, for instance, helps explain to the MIT students why the notions of freedom and equality are viewed as inseparable by the French. This is something MIT students had already noticed when they had analyzed the French responses to the words *freedom* and *liberté* and had observed that words such as *limitée, autrui,* and *égalité* kept recurring on the French side. That very close connection between the notions of *égalité* and of *liberté* becomes even more apparent to the American students if they happen to read Article 4 of the *Déclaration des Droits de l'Homme* (in the library module), which says: "La liberté consiste à pouvoir faire tout ce qui ne nuit pas à autrui: ainsi, l'exercise des droits naturels de chaque homme n'a de bornes que celles qui assurent aux autres membres de la société la jouissance de ces mêmes droits." (Freedom consists in being able to do everything that is not harmful to others: consequently, the only limits to the exercise of each man's natural rights are those that guarantee the other members of society the enjoyment of those same rights.)

In *Teaching and Assessing Intercultural Communicative Competence,* Michael Byram defines what a true intercultural speaker is (we can substitute here the word *reader*):

> The intercultural speaker can "read" a document or event, analyzing its origin and sources—e.g., in the media, in political speech or historical writing—and the meanings and values which arise from a national or other ethnocentric perspective (stereotypes, historical connotations in texts) and which are presupposed and implicit, leading to conclusions which can be challenged from a different perspective.

> The intercultural speaker can identify causes of misunderstanding (e.g., use of concepts apparently similar but with different meanings or connotations . . . the intercultural speaker can use . . . explanations of sources of misunderstanding and dysfunction to help interlocutors overcome conflicting perspectives [and] can explain the perspective of each and the origins of those perspectives in terms accessible to the other. (Byram 1997, p. 61)

I believe that our *Cultura* students, having honed their skills at reading between the cultural lines, are well on their way to becoming, as Byram writes, literate intercultural readers.

References

Bahktin, M. (1986). *Speech Genres and Other Late Essays,* edited by Caryl Emerson and Michael Holquist and translated by Vern W. McGee. Austin: University of Texas Press.

Byram, M. (1997). *Teaching and Assessing Intercultural Communicative Competence.* Clevedon, U.K.: Multilingual Matters.

De Tocqueville, A. (1961). *De la démocratie en Amérique.* Paris: Gallimard, Folio Histoire.

Makine, A. (1995). *Le Testament français.* Paris: Gallimard Folio Histoire. *Dreams of My Russian Summers,* translated by Geoffrey Strachan. New York: Arcade, 1997.

APPENDIX: FORUMS ON THE WORD ASSOCIATION EXERCISE FOR
INDIVIDUALISM/INDIVIDUALISME, FALL 1999

Alexis N—12:44pm Oct 12, 1999 (#1 of 16)

Visiblement notre conception du mot individualism ou individualisme n'est
pas du tout la meme! En effet en France, celui-ci a un sens plutot pejoratif tres
associe au sens du mot egoisme. Pour vous, il semble plutot que ce soit la consideration naturelle envers un individu, un mot associe au sens de liberte individuelle.
En France, on est plus enclin a s'interesser au groupe et l'individu a moins de
place au niveau du langage, je pense cependant que l'individualisme est largement
present en France, meme si on l'avoue peut-etre plus difficilement. Comment
definiriez-vous le mot individualism, comment le vivez-vous?

Marine T—02:34pm Oct 12, 1999 (#2 of 16)

bonjour! j'ai observé nos réponses à propos du mot individualisme, et il
semble qu'aux Etats-Unis, cela semble revendiqué comme une valeur américaine,
liée à l'intégrité, alors qu'en France, cela est plutôt considéré comme un comportement malsaint. Je crois en fait que nous n'avons pas la même idée de ce qu'est
l'individualisme, et cela à cause de nos différences culturelles. Ainsi, pour les américains, l'esprit d'initiative est très valorisé et je trouve cela très bien, mais ne pensez-
vous pas que le travail de groupe est aussi très enrichissant?

Anne-Laure L—05:47am Oct 13, 1999 (#3 of 16)

La difference entre les deux conceptions de l'individualisme est en effet tres
nette. Si en France, l'individualisme est percu comme de l'egoisme ou une fermeture au monde, aux Etats-Unis, il permet d'affirmer sa difference et de construire sa
liberte par des choix. Cette notion est donc naturellement liee aux Etats-Unis et au
capitalisme. Peut-etre cette difference est-elle due a l'histoire des Etats-Unis, nation
plus recente, ou les autodidactes sont encourages, tout comme l'esprit d'initiative,
dans la creation d'entreprises ou en recherche par exemple. Par contre, je ne saia pas
si l'individualisme americain se fait au detriment de l'esprit de groupe, qui ne me
semble pas tellement plus encourage en France.

Amelie S—06:35am Oct 13, 1999 (#4 of 16)

Nos différences de conception du mot individualisme sont flagrantes. Nous
associons individualime à égoisme et égocentrisme, l'individualiste est pour nous
celui qui marche sur les autres pour progresser tandis que pour vous il s'agit de
liberté. En fait, vos comportements sociaux sont très différents des nôtres, même si
l'écart semble s'atténuer un peu ces dernières années, tant aux niveau de la vie en
entreprise que dans la vie de tous les jours. Je pense que cette différence fondamen-
tale est due à nos bagages historiques et politiques respectifs. L'individualisme est
pour nous un comportement méprisé au profit peut-être de la solidarité et de
l'esprit d'équipe. Qu'en est-t'il de ces valeurs chez vous?

Laurent J—10:25am Oct 13, 1999 (#5 of 16)

Les self-made men ne sont pas monnaie courante en France. Pour nous, la seule entite capable de fournir des resultats probants est une equipe d'individus dans laquelle on peut eventuellement trouver une certaine competition, qui peut a la rigueur pousser a un comportement individualiste. L'individualisme est apprecie uniquement dans ce cas, au sein d'une competition amicale. J'ai l'impression que vous assimilez l'individualisme a une espece d'originalite, tres loin de tout esprit de competition. Ne pensez-vous pas que la competition, la concurrence pure et dure, coute trop chere?

Michael W—04:32pm Oct 13, 1999 (#6 of 16)

En france, "individualisme" a une connotation très négative, alors qu'aux Etats-Unis, le mot a une consonnace très positive. Par ailleurs, la notion d'individualisme semble être, pour les américains, parfaitement assumée: c'est un "choix" lié à une volonté de se démarquer, d'affirmer sa liberté . . . Manifestement, nous n'avons pas la même définition du mot "individualisme." C'est sans doute plus un problème de vocabulaire que de culture, car je ne crois pas que l' "égoïsme," ou la "fermeture d'esprit" (associations que font les français) soient des qualités aux Etats-Unis. L'individualisme au sens américain du terme se rapprocherait plutôt de ce que nous appelons le "développement personnel" ou l'affirmation de soi.

Alexis C—06:38pm Oct 13, 1999 (#7 of 16)

Le terme Individualisme a une signification très différente en France et aux Etats-Unis. Du côté français, l'individualisme n'a visiblement pas le succés qu'il a aux Etats-Unis. L'individualisme est considéré comme un défaut par les français car ils semblent considérer l'individualisme comme une sorte de manière de tout vouloir pour soi (égoïsme est très souvent cité). Les Etats-Unis et le modèle capitaliste sont aussi rattachés au terme individualisme par les Français, ce qui semble être vérifié quand on considère que les Américains voient l'individualisme comme important et comme une manière de vivre et de se sentir libre et différent des autres. Les Américains semblent ne pas accepter d'être absorbés par la masse.

Catherine K N—02:56am Oct 14, 1999 (#8 of 16)

Hi everyone! When I first read the words all of you used associating to "individualism" I felt completely shocked. The ideal that Americans hold so closely to themselves is scorned by another country! It is so fascinating that we have such different interpretations of the "same" word! =) I think that the main difference between our usage of the two words involves the context in which we derive it from. For you in France, "individualisme" focuses on the idea that the person believes that he or she could do anything and everything by himself or herself. In the U.S., we simply call the person an egotist. Slang terms for that would include "smart aleck," "wise guy," and "know-it all." An egotist is also looked badly upon here. "Individualism" in our terms means independence. The connotation concentrates on the idea that a person does not need to and should not conform to all the ideas other people have. Everyone should think for himself or herself. It is important to us not to have to depend on others for everything. A few of you mentioned the idea of group work as well. We believe that group work is a good thing. An egotist would not participate in a group because he/she would think that he/she is too good and smart for the group. Yet an individual would work in a group because he/she can share their individually thought up ideas with the group to result in more ideas generated. I don't personally know how this word's meaning changed so drastically through history. But I do think that it has a lot to do with the way the U.S. developed into a country. When the colonies were under British rules, most of the normal people did as they were told. But a few individuals realized that people deserved better so they got together and shared their ideas and ideals. That eventually led to a revolution and the rest is history. Perhaps at one time, those few individuals were seen as egotists trying to do something completely crazy. Maybe because they succeeded, the term individualism slowly developed in a more positive light. Or maybe I am completely wrong with that idea. =)

Matthew R F—08:34am Oct 14, 1999 (#9 of 16)

I agree with Catherine that how the countries developed has a lot to do with the connotations and some to do with the denotations of individualism. As she mentioned, the United States grew out of a desire to be independent from Britain where as France grew out out of a desire for equality for all. The French revolution resulted in the removal of nobles with an unequal share of rights and privileges. Americans view individualism as growing above your environment to be the most you can.

Dmitry S N—06:01pm Oct 14, 1999 (#10 of 16)

Having read the previous responses, I realized that 'there is no p̄roblem'—we simply understand the word 'individualism' differently. They are like two different words for you and us, though they happen to be spelled similarly. My question then is, how do you call the person who evidently pursues his or her career, is not afraid of taking decisions, develops his/her personality etc? Also, from my experience with Western Europe (I studied there for a year and have been there many times), it seems that people there try to eliminate/diminish competition, or at least not to notice it. What is the attitude in whatever group of people (same class at school, same company) to anyone who obviously tries to go beyond, works harder, tries to succeed? Do you start respecting him/her more, or vice-versa, think about such person as 'someone who wants too much', 'shows off', 'thinking only about career' etc?

Miranda L P—06:28pm Oct 17, 1999 (#11 of 16)

In response to Marine, I think that the United States does praise individualism, however not at the expense of teamwork. Especially in education, teamwork is considered vital to learning. I don't think that the two have to be considered opposing ideas. Like Catherine said, individualism can exist within a group. Individualism as Americans know it goes beyond "being an individual." It also has a lot to do with finding value in the ideas of man and seeing the power to change that each person has.

Claudiu A G—02:31am Oct 18, 1999 (#12 of 16)

I see that for French "individualisme" means acting for oneself and being selfish. Obviously, in US, the word having a close spelling means acting by oneself and having one's own way. I was wondering (since these words have a common root, "individual") if in France referring to a person as an "individual" has somehow a negative connotation. To answer Marine: Working in groups is definitely a good thing. I'm thinking of study groups, for example, which are quite popular at MIT (although not allowed by some courses). When solving a problem of general interest say for a company working in a group is a requirement. However, shaping one's own career (to illustrate the positive connotation of individualism) cannot be a group activity.

Christine A K—03:15am Oct 18, 1999 (#13 of 16)

Hmm . . . do you think that the people in charge paired individualisme with individualism on purpose to create conflict in our responses? I suspect so . . . I think it is interesting to uncover the quirks and little differences in languages. History really does shade meanings and connotations of words.

And in response to Alexis, when I read what you said about Americans not wanting to be absorbed into the masses, I shuddered. That sounds really horrible. I think that most people like to stand out as individuals and to be seen for the unique people they are. Correct me if I'm wrong, but I think that "conformity" has a very negative connotation in the US. Is this the same in France?

Christian B—09:48am Oct 18, 1999 (#14 of 16)

Réactions aux réponses sur l'individualisme. D'emblée on constate que les Américains ont une vision globalement positive de la notion d'individualisme (à 92%), tandis que les français la considère plutôt négativement. On notera ensuite que hormis l'indépendance et l'égocentrisme, aucune des réponses proposées n'est commune aux 2 pays. Ainsi, du côté des réponses positives, les français décrivent l'individualisme d'un point de vue "institutionnel" (capitalisme, libéralisme, indépendance, liberté), tandis que les Américains se situent dans une logique plus "personnelle." L'individualisme n'est dès lors pas un comportement propre à un ensemble social ou le fruit d'une doctrine, mais le fruit d'une décision personnelle, justement en rupture avec la société, comme en témoignent les réponses mode de vie, anticonformisme, choix. En revanche, lorsqu'il s'agit des aspects négatifs les français se situent au niveau strictement individuel. L'individualiste devient alors un être égocentrique, solitaire et fermé d'esprit.

Ludovic M—10:27am Oct 18, 1999 (#15 of 16)

Effectivement, je pense que Matthew nous offre une très bonne synthèse, qui explique simplement nos différences quant à l'appréhension de l'individualisme. Il y a, je pense, à prendre des deux côtés: nous aurions à gagner en France à laisser développer l'imagination, la créativité des individus; mais il y a, aux US, un "revers de médaillon": à trop vouloir pousser l'individualisme, il me semble qu'on s'isole toujours un peu plus, et, même si l'on peut au début affirmer la force de son entité, l'on arrive à mal vivre son unicité. Partager, communiquer et échanger pour s'enrichir de l'expérience des autres, on peut aussi le faire de façon unique.

Liana F L—11:46am Oct 18, 1999 (#16 of 16)

As has been said, we obviously have very different ideas of what the word means. MIT students in particular tend to be the people who were the outsiders in their high school, because they did better in classes and sometimes weren't so popular. I think that among some other groups in America, individualism is not seen so positively. There are many stories of people who have different opinions, different fashions, etc, being considered wrong or dangerous by their communities (schools, town, and so on). So I don't think that every American would agree that individualism is a good characteristic, even though it is very important to me.

6

Reading and Technology in Less Commonly Taught Languages and Cultures

MASAKO UEDA FIDLER

Preliminaries: Reading Forms in Discourse and in Cultural Contexts

Interpreting a text is one of the most important components of language learning. Although it is a complicated procedure for any learner, it is especially challenging for students of less commonly taught languages. Most of these require a large amount of time to reach a certain point of proficiency. A teacher must spend much classroom time on formal aspects of these languages, such as various inflectional forms and complexities of the writing system. The fact that these languages are often not taught below the college level exacerbates the situation. Thus, when students of more commonly taught languages may be capable of discussing literature or politics relatively soon after entering college, students of Czech or Japanese may be struggling to talk about their daily activities and to make simple statements about their preferences.

This is not to say that students of less commonly taught languages do not learn culture at the beginning level. They do become aware of differences in worldview reflected in language in different ways: for example, how to express simple sensations (use of the dative case for the experiencer in Czech) and wants or impositions (the third-person *-garu* in Japanese), to present an event with a focus on completion or on the occurrence of an action itself (verbal aspect in Czech), or to report acts of giving and receiving (giving and receiving verbs in Japanese). Because of the structural complexities of the languages and time constraints, however, reading in these languages tends to focus only on micro-level properties of a text: understanding the morphological features of each constituent and syntactic relation.

In this chapter I shall attempt to show that a full interpretation of a text requires consideration of not only micro-level elements but also macro-level elements, namely, discourse strategies and historical and cultural contexts. A cross-linguistic comparison of such strategies and contexts also belongs to analysis on the macro level. I shall discuss how apparently puzzling micro-level properties of a text can be interpreted fully once cultural and historical context is incorporated into the reading process. Some of the examples will suggest that reading based solely on micro-level properties may lead to misguided interpretation of a text. I shall then go back to the issue of teaching materials for Czech as an example of a less commonly taught language, discuss the significance of electronic materials and the Web, and propose possible ingredients for them.

Interpretation of Texts as a Complex Process

In order to show the significance of both micro- and macro-level aspects of language in interpreting texts, I shall use samples from three speakers from different cultures: former president Bill Clinton, President Vaclav Havel of the Czech Republic, and former prime minister Yoshiro Mori of Japan. All three political leaders reflect on events and accomplishments of the preceding year and the challenges of the new year, and all address their reflections to citizens of their countries. I do not intend to evaluate or analyze the political abilities of these speakers. Rather, I wish to demonstrate the complexities of the interaction between structural properties of texts and sociocultural contexts, more specifically, how certain structural properties of texts might be effectively interpreted when we consider discourse/pragmatic norm and sociohistorical context both within a language and cross-linguistically. The features discussed here roughly correspond to what Fairclough defines as "relational values" of these texts (1989, 112). Relational values, according to Fairclough, constitute one of the three values that are found in a political text. They represent "trace of/cue to social relationships enacted in a text." This includes expression of power or authority and rapport-building.

Reading on the Micro Level

Let us first examine some of the micro-level properties of the three speeches: sentence-level surface forms such as modifiers and predicates, including politeness forms and modal expressions. We shall then consider potential interpretations that may arise if the texts are interpreted merely on the sentence level.

One of the salient features of Clinton's speech, compared to that of the other two, is that it has the highest frequency of the first-person singular forms. I-forms—here and elsewhere, boldface is used to highlight the structural features under discussion—are most frequently associated with verbs of asking (for support) and proposing and tend to be repeated in a pattern:

> (1) . . . **I ask** you to pass a real patients' bill of rights. [Applause] **I ask** you to pass common-sense gun safety legislation. [Applause] **I ask** you to pass campaign finance reform. [Applause] . . . And, again, **I ask** you—**I implore** you—to raise the minimum wage. [Applause] (1/27/00)

Such sentences are preceded by a premise that is presented as a majority view. They are often accompanied by applause explicitly noted in the transcript in order to accentuate that many people agree with the speaker:

> (2) **We know** that children learn best in smaller classes with good teachers. . . . **Congress has supported my plan** to hire 100,000 new qualified teachers to lower class size in the early grades. **I thank** you for that, and **I ask** you to make it three in a row. [Applause] (1/27/00)

Such a combination of predicate types and I-forms is in agreement with the expected function of the U.S. president: advising the Congress of his perception of the nation's needs and, as head of the executive branch, obtaining support from others to realize his visions.

Clinton's speeches are also rich in first-person plural forms:

> (3) **We will bring** prosperity to every American community. . . . And **we will become** at last what **our** founders pledged **us** to be so long ago—one nation, under God, indivisible, with liberty and justice for all. [Applause] These are great goals, worthy of a great nation. (1/27/00)

The speaker uses them to emphasize previous and ongoing accomplishments and future projects, presenting himself and the audience as a successful team:

> (4) Crime in America has dropped for the past seven years—that's the longest decline on record—thanks to **a national consensus** we helped forge on community police, sensible gun safety laws, and effective prevention. [Applause] (1/27/00)

These forms help engage the audience as respected members of the political leadership. When the speaker, his administration, the Congress, or all the American people are referred to as one entity, the speaker's ability to collaborate with various people despite apparent differences is being accentuated. This observation is consistent with the frequent use of words such as "bipartisan" and "working together."

In contrast, Prime Minister Mori's approach does not explicitly utilize first-person plural forms. Although it is somewhat similar to Clinton's approach in that both speakers use first-person singular references with verbs of proposing and asking, Mori's style is marked by frequent use of politeness markers, especially humble forms of self-reference.

> (5) Kyooikukihonhoo ni tuite mo bapponteki ni minaosu hituyoo ga aru to kangaete **ori**masu. . . . omoikitta kaikaku wo sekkyokuteki ni suisin site **mairi**masu. (7/28/2000) (I also think [**humbly**] that there is a need to drastically review the Basic Law on Education. . . . I will actively [**humbly**] promote bold reforms on the basis of national debate.)

These forms might be interpreted as the speaker's markedly respectful attitude toward the audience; he is, as it were, humbly presenting the plans of his Cabinet, "serving" the country, and imploring the audience to support him.

As for Havel's speeches, first-person references are connected for the most part with processes of thinking, believing, or knowing.

> (6) **Věřím,** že nadcházející rok přinese nové impulzy . . . (1/1/95)
> (**I believe** that the coming year will bring new impulses . . .)

> (7) **Nevím,** zda život jako takový je či není hezký. **Vím** ale, že je velkou výzvou pro každého z nás, aby se ho pokusil udělat hezkým sobě a ostatním. (1/1/98)
> (**I do not know** whether life as such is or is not beautiful. **I know,** however, that it is a great challenge for every one of us to try to make it beautiful for oneself and for others.)

As did Clinton, Havel also uses first-person plural forms to report past accomplishments in reference to himself and the entire audience:

> (8) Jasně **jsme se přihlásili** k humanistické a demokratické tradici naší novodobé historie. (1/1/94)
> (**We declared our allegiance** to the humanistic and democratic traditions of our recent history.)

There are, however, a large number of situations associated with first-person plural subjects that are simply descriptive or even negative:

(9) Zbořili jsme sice už dávno velkou zed, která nás oddělovala od demokratické Evropy, ale zároveň **tolerujeme,** že kolem nás a mezi námi zvolna a nenápadně vyrůstají zdi nové. (1/1/99)
(Granted, we already tore down the great wall which separated us from the democratic Europe, but simultaneously **we tolerate** that new walls are slowly and inconspicuously growing around us and among us.)

These forms present the audience in relation to the speaker as political co-players, but not necessarily in a positive light; instead, they emphasize that both the audience and the speaker are equally accountable for various consequences. The prominence of words such as *odpovědnost* (responsibility), *odpovědný* (responsible), *spoluodpovědnost* (co-responsibility), and *spoluodpovědný* (co-responsible) in Havel's speeches supports this observation.

The examples from Clinton's speech represent the president as a man of action who makes proposals based on the values accepted by a majority of people, who respects the audience as his successful partners, and who is capable of working with everyone to achieve what's good for the country and of overcoming apparent differences. In contrast, the other two speakers seem to exhibit properties that are different or puzzzling. The Japanese prime minister might produce an image of a very polite leader of a state who serves the nation with humility. Havel's texts may be somewhat puzzling to the reader because they speak about his opinions rather than concrete plans and challenges for the coming year. The reader may also wonder why he should admit that he holds not only his citizens but also himself responsible for negative conditions. For public relations purposes, this may appear strategically ineffective.

Such readings of texts by Havel and Mori seem reasonable on the sentence level. They would certainly be attractive to the reader who is looking for something distinct about other cultures such as a relatively unknown central European state and a country in Asia with different values and codes of behavior. In fact, further examples may appear to confirm these views.

Reading Havel on the Micro Level

Let us first look at Havel's texts more closely on the sentence level. Havel's modal verbs of obligation are used to suggest that the current situation is not ideal. Such an interpretation is possible especially when modal verbs are negated (see Givon 1979, p. 139 on negation):

(10) **Nesmí** nám být jedno, co se děje kolem nás, jakou tvář má naše země a její krajina, naše města a obce; **nemůžeme** myslet jen na to, abychom měli

dobrý dům a garáž, ale musíme myslet i na to, co je obklopuje; **nemůžeme** hájit jen zájmy své firmy či svého povolání. (1/1/00)
(We **must not** be indifferent to what happens around us; or to the face of our country, of its landscape, of its towns and villages; we **must not** think only about having a fine house and garage of our own, but also about that which surrounds them; we **cannot** defend solely the interests of our own company or our profession.)

The reader might wonder why a president of a state criticizes the current situation when he—as a major part of the political machinery—is responsible for it. In contrast, modal expressions in Clinton's speech are often accompanied by an implicitly positive prognosis:

(11) Now, as we demand more from our schools, we **should** also invest more in our schools. [Applause] . . . **If** we do this, we **can** give every single child in every failing school in America—everyone—the chance to meet high standards. (1/27/00)

Compare (11) with (12), in which Havel warns that some negative consequences might follow should a wrong step be taken:

(12) Duch zdí může mít nakonec jediný důsledek: **nenápadné ochromení tak důležitých údů demokracie,** jakými jsou princip občanské rovnosti, úcta k nezcizitelným lidským právům . . . (1/1/99)
(The spirit of the wall can have after all one consequence: **inconspicuous paralysis of such important limbs of democracy** as the principle of equality of citizens, respect for inalienable human rights . . .)

Another interesting feature of Havel's use of modality is that its "source" (Chung and Timberlake 1990, pp. 241–42), or entity that expresses obligations or necessity, is primarily the speaker. He is the individual who believes that certain situations should hold. He is the individual who believes that other situations are not acceptable. Compare (12) with (13), in which the speaker's political programs are assumed to be in accord with a widely established value, the concept of the American Revolution:

(13) We will bring prosperity to every American community. . . . And we will become at last **what our founders pledged us to be** so long ago—**one nation, under God, indivisible, with liberty and justice for all.** [Applause] These are great goals, **worthy of a great nation.** (1/27/00)

The nature of modality is therefore significantly different in Havel's and Clinton's speeches; Havel presents himself as the major source of modality, whereas Clinton spreads his modality over a group of people, presenting himself as a team player. Furthermore, Havel's speeches contain modal expressions that suggest the existence of others who may not share his view. Note the implicit contrast in (14) and (15):

> (14) Je to úkol všech veřejně činných lidí, všech lidí v odpovědních postaveních a koneckonců všech nás, občanů České republiky, **kteří to s ní myslíme dobře.** (1/1/00)
> (It is a task for all people involved in public activities; for all those holding responsible positions; and, actually, for all of us—citizens of the Czech Republic **who mean well for this country.**)

> (15) Sám sobě i nám všem nejlépe pomůže **ten z nás, kdo bude . . . volit vskutku odpovědně** . . . (1/1/98)
> (**One who votes in a truly responsible manner** . . . will help oneself and all of us most.)

Examples (16) and (17) suggest the existence of influential people who are slumbering instead of acting. Example (17) suggests the existence of people who may vary in the degree to which they must confront difficulties in maintaining high moral principles.

> (16) Musíme ji [naději] naplňovat sami. Byť třeba i tím, že zatřeseme všemi, **kteří mají sice vliv, ale dřímají, místo aby jednali.** (1/1/00)
> (We have to fulfill it [hope] ourselves. Perhaps, among other things, by shaking up all those **who possess influence but slumber instead of acting.**)

> (17) Všem **takovýmto** lidem patří dík. **Dík tím větší, oč větší jsou nesnáze, které musejí překonávat.** (1/1/94)
> (All **such** people deserve our gratitude and **the greater the difficulties they must overcome, the greater our gratitude should be.**)

The reader may again wonder why a politican even hints at the fact that not everyone agrees with him. One may think that Havel is speaking defensively.

Havel's speeches are also marked by a unique way of referring to individuals in the third person. Such forms in Havel's speeches are much more anonymous than in the speeches of the other two speakers, often including indefinite expressions such as *někdo* (someone) and *někteří* (some people).

> (18) Vím ale, na co právo mám: podělit se s vámi—byť by to **někdo** stokrát nazval moralizováním—o svůj názor na to . . . (1/1/00)
> (But I know what I have the right to do: I can—even though **some** may dismiss it as a mere moralizing a hundred times over—share with you my opinion . . .)

People, who are technically sources of information, are not directly mentioned in Havel's speeches; instead, abstract nouns are used:

(19) **Různé průzkumy veřejného mínění říkají, že** . . . (1/1/99)
(**Various polls of public opinion say that** . . .)

(20) **Některé odhady říkají, že** . . . (1/1/00)
(**Some estimates say that** . . .)

(21) O všech těchto a dalších civilizačních hrozbách ví dnešní lidstvo velmi dobře, vždyť **se tím zabývají samostatné vědní obory, mnohé světové konference** . . . (1/1/00)
(Humanity knows very well about all these and other threats to our civilization, after all, **independent disciplines of science, many global conferences deal with this** . . .)

Conversely, abstract notions tend to be personified in Havel's speeches:

(22) A tak **se** tu znovu **hlásí ke slovu** naše známé a sebeničivé **čecháčkovství.** (1/1/99)
(And so here again our well known and self-destructive **Czech-narrow mindedness claims the floor.**)

(23) V prostředí plotů, dělících čar a nedůvěřivého či pohrdavého vztahu k jakékoli jinakosti bývají ovšem takové vlastnosti jako laskavost, vlídnost, nezištnost či bezelstná upřímnost předmětem tichého posměchu. **Cynismu, kariérismu, závisti, zbabělosti a zlobě—zvlášť jsou-li zahaleny do svatouškovského hávu—se** v něm naopak **daří.** (1/1/99)
(In the milieu of fences, dividing lines, and suspicious or contemptuous relations to any sort of otherness, of course, properties such as benevolence, kindness, unselfishness, or sincere honesty are often the object of a silent ridicule. **Cynicism, selfish career-mindedness, envy, cowardice, and malice—** especially **if they are clad in a sanctimonious robe—**on the contrary, **do well** in it [this milieu].)

Compare these examples with Clinton's third-person references. Clinton's speeches refer to concrete individuals in conjunction with their positive accomplishments:

(24) Mr. Speaker, it was a powerful moment last November when **you** joined Reverend Jesse Jackson and me in **your** home state of Illinois and committed to working toward our common goal, by combining the best ideas from both sides of the aisle. I want to thank **you** again and to tell **you, Mr. Speaker,** I look forward to working with **you.** This is a worthy, joint endeavor. Thank you. [Applause] (1/27/00)

In reporting sources of information, some referents are semianonymous but nonetheless descriptive:

(25) For example, **researchers** have identified genes . . . **Researchers** already are using this new technique . . . **Scientists** are also working on an artificial retina to help many blind people to see. (1/1/00)

Such devices create an impression that the speaker is working and consulting with specialists. This is another way to present oneself as a co-player. The process of self-presentation is therefore strikingly distinct in Havel's speeches compared to Clinton's. The scarcity of references to specific individuals other than the speaker tends to present Havel the president as the sole source of modality and reliable information. The president can be viewed as reporting to the potentially misinformed audience what is truly a democratic society. Without considering the macro-level properties of the text, Havel's approach may seem puzzling to a reader who is accustomed to hearing political speeches like Clinton's in which the speaker presents not only himself but also the audience and others as individuals who know what is best for the country.

Reading Mori on the Micro Level

Mori's speeches also seem to exhibit a set of unusual properties on the sentence level. As mentioned above, Mori tends to refer to his contacts with various groups of people rather than distinct individuals. His speech strategies differ from both Clinton's and Havel's in his use of humble and honorific forms (indicated in parentheses); he not only takes the position of a subordinate in relation to the communities (26) but also sometimes assumes the role of a superior in relation to certain groups of people as in (27):

(26) Konkai no samitto kaisai ni saisi, jimoto hukuoka, miyazaki, okinawa no **katagata,** sosite zenkoku no minasama kara tadai no gosien, gojinryoku wo **itadakimasita.** kokorokara orei **moosiagemasu.** (4/7/00)
Toward the hosting of the Summit Meeting, I (**humbly**) received (**honorable**) support and (**honorable**) help from **the (respected) people** of the local Fukuoka, Miyazaki, and Okinawa and all (respected) people of the entire country. I **humbly express** thanks from the bottom of my heart.

(27) Koomuin **syokun** ni taisite wa senpan sikoo sareta kokka koomuin rinrihoo wo humae kooki no gensei to rinri no koojoo ni torikumuyoo tuyoku **motomemasu.** (4/7/00)
Toward the public servants (**who are my subordinates**), **I demand** that they strive for propriety in their actions and for an improvement in their ethics, in line with the recently promulgated National Public Official Moral Code.

The speaker thus indicates his position in a hierarchy in which he presents himself as a superordinate to public servants and as a subordinate to ordinary citizens.

Another salient feature of Mori's speeches can be found in his references to predecessors or ancestors (*senjin*) as a source of modality.

> (28) Watasitati wa **senjintati** no ketui to doryoku ni omoi wo itasi nagara, atarasii seiki no nippon . . . wo tukutte **ikanakereba narimasen.** (7/2/00)
> (Ever mindful of the determination and efforts of **our predecessors,** we **must** build a nation for the new century.)

The speaker also positions himself as having been chosen by providence:

> (29) Obutizensoori no kookeisya ni watasi ga erabareta koto wa **tenmei** da to uketomete orimasu. (4/7/00)
> (I [humbly] choose to view the fact that I have been chosen as a successor of former Prime Minister Obuchi as **an act of providence.**)

Mori thus seems to be humbly accepting a leadership position assigned by higher forces.

Mori's texts may further catch the reader's eye with their apparently poetic and almost romantic visions of Japan's future:

> (30) watasi wa honnaikaku wo **"nippon sinsei naikaku"** to site, **"ansin site yume wo motte kuraseru kokka," "kokoro no yutaka na utukusii kokka," "sekai kara sinrai sareru kokka,"** sonoyoona kokka no jitugen wo mezasite mairimasu. (4/7/00)
> (I christen [lit., make] this administration the **"Cabinet for the Rebirth of Japan"** and will [humbly] aim to realize **"a nation of people who live in security embracing our dreams for the future," "a nation of beauty rich in spirit,"** and **"a nation that engenders the trust of the world."**

Linguistic devices such as politeness markers and ways of presenting himself and his political programs make Mori appear to be a humble and polite public servant, at least on the surface.

A Second Look at Structural Properties and Speech Strategies in Context

It is convenient to consider these apparently unusual linguistic patterns as direct manifestations of cultural differences. One may even state at this stage that we can learn to appreciate such cultural differences. We could compare these features and create a linguistic or cultural typology. I would like to question, however, whether these approaches lead to cultivating understanding and appreciation of languages and cultures.

I shall look more closely at the texts, this time with attention to both the micro-level and macro-level properties: how sentence-level properties interact with discourse and social contexts (when the speeches are delivered, how and where they are delivered, and the audience to whom they were delivered). I shall then reveal greater similarities between Mori and Clinton in spite of differences on the micro level. Motivations for what appear to be puzzling features can be explained after we consider Havel's historical and political experience.

As mentioned above, Mori's speeches may give the impression that the speaker is an unusually polite public servant when the text is analyzed without attention to discourse-level properties. Examination of the structural properties of the language *used in the particular context* shows, however, that this is not entirely an accurate description.

True, as seen above, in Mori's speeches humble forms abound. He emphasizes his dedication to his country. Note, however, that humble forms are on-the-record (Brown and Levinson 1987, pp. 17–21) politeness markers. They are nearly automatic in such speeches. When translated literally, these forms may seem to contain excessive degrees of politeness, as in (26) and (27), but they are semirequired components of contemporary politicians' speeches. More important, these forms compensate for the absence of explicit first-person plural forms in speeches that would otherwise express solidarity with the addressee. In other words, the politeness markers are used not only as a norm but also for a political purpose: to engage the audience and win its support. For this reason, it is also necessary for the speaker to present himself as holding all the branches of his government under his control; hence the use of forms expressing the speaker's superiority over the government officials.

Another similarity between Clinton and Mori can be seen in the predicate semantics associated with the first-person singular references. Clinton's predicates do not necessarily report actions in the sense of causing something to materialize without failure, as in (1) and (2). Specific visions are being proposed, but the speaker does not guarantee their realization. A similar type of predicate is frequently found in Mori's speeches: verbs emphasizing maximum effort and strong determination.

> (31) Moteru **tikara no kagiri wo tukusi, sinmei wo tosite** kokusei ni tori-kunde mairimasu. (4/7/00)
> (I will [humbly] **apply [lit., exhaust] my full strength** and tackle the matters of state, **devoting [lit., risking] my body and life.**)

(32) . . . korekara no nippon no tame ni toomen suru syokadai ni **kenmei ni torikumi** . . . (7/28/00)
(. . .**to channel all my efforts** into tackling . . . the challenges we face for the sake of our future Japan)

These verbs could be interpreted as metaphorically reporting causality (transferring his power into some project). They therefore may appear to present the prime minister's strong dedication. The verbs, however, leave the causality between the speaker's effort and the realization of his intended projects opaque. Mori's speeches create an image of a politician who is actively involved in his duties, but his predicates avoid guaranteeing that his visions will materialize.

There are also similarities between Mori's and Clinton's texts in the way their political programs are proposed. Clinton draws support for his programs from people other than himself: groups of experts—members of Congress in (2) and (24), scientists as in (25), and valuers of the spirit of American democratic values, as in (3). His political programs, in other words, are presented as being based on consensus and on democratic principles that are nearly indisputable in the American social context. Mori's references to the wisdom of his ancestors in (28) and divine forces in (29)—entities that automatically deserve respect in the Japanese social context—justify his position and his programs. Nominalization of Mori's political visions in (30) blurs the timing of processes (Fairclough 1989, p. 124) and helps them appear as axioms. This observation is consistent with other features of Mori's texts. Mori often embeds modal expressions in subordinate clauses that modify nouns; this device results in an interpretation that the stated necessity and obligation already are established facts. Modal expressions also occur in relative clauses that modify nouns. Here, too, modality is not questioned but is presented as an established value:

(33) Zaiseikoozoo kaikaku ga kanarazu jitugen sin**akerebanaranai** juuyoo-kadai de arukoto wa ron wo matimasen. (4/7/00)
(There is no doubt whatsoever that fiscal structural reform is a matter of utmost priority that **must** absolutely be achieved.)

Clinton's and Mori's speeches start with a premise on which everyone is said to agree. Then concrete political plans based on this premise are proposed. Each speaker presents the audience as a team player with the intention of having his program approved. Realization of the plans, the degree to which the plans reflect the premise, and the actual definition of the premise are left ambiguous. In addition, the speaker does not need to take full responsibility for the premise because it results from commonly accepted values or traditions. It is then possible that the speaker will not be held entirely accountable for the political program based on this premise.

Clearly, the speeches by Clinton and Mori, in spite of their apparent structural differences, use similar discourse strategies to promote political plans. The present data set, in spite of its small size, indicates that a text must be interpreted not only in terms of sentence-level properties (for example, expression of politeness) but also in terms of speech registers (for example, political speech) using both internal and comparative approaches.

In contrast to the speeches of these two speakers, Havel's do not contain political programs. This is partially due to his political function as head of state rather than as head of the executive branch. The absence of concrete political programs and references to concrete achievements in the preceding year, however, is also connected with what used to be contained in New Year's Addresses in socialist Czechoslovakia. Havel's texts can be seen as reactions to the texts by his predecessors, who presented positive accomplishments of the socialist state, especially production of steel, wheat, and other food products and future political programs such as five-year plans. This interpretation is consistent with Havel's own statement that he does not want to introduce numbers because he thinks that the audience must be tired of hearing such things in New Year's Addresses. Thus, the apparently unusual style of Havel's political speeches is constructed on another layer of political speeches. This is not surprising considering his sensitivity to how texts can be deformed and made into utter nonsense, as shown in his play *Vyrozumění* (*The Memorandum*, 1966). With still-vivid memories of a typical speech under the totalitarian regime, the speaker intentionally takes the diametrically opposite approach.

Unlike a typical socialist speechmaker, Havel strives to convince the audience of the validity of his beliefs. His speeches, in other words, involve a debate or a dialogue:

> (34) **Vím, jak to zní nepopulárně, ale nemohu si pomoct:** nejvíc ublížíme sami sobě, když se budeme starat jen sami o sebe. (1/1/00)
> (**I know how unpopular it sounds, but I cannot help telling you this:** We will hurt ourselves most if we care about nothing but ourselves.)

In order to provoke, persuade, and convince the audience, Havel tends to present himself as the major source of authority—of modality and evaluation. It is also important to modify the addressee's potential misguided beliefs by zooming in on their negative properties. Rhetorical questions may also be used to challenge the addressee in this regard:

(35) Ano, kdo jiný je tvůrcem hodnot, než svobodný člověk? Ale **cožpak je
člověk jen tímto?** (1/1/97)
(True, who but a free human being is the creator of values? **But is this all that
there is in humanity?**)

Havel's texts question rather than present concepts such as democracy and
freedom as axioms. In this style of argumentation, it is necessary to contrast
the speaker's belief and the audience's possible misguided belief. The speaker
needs to show that the latter would lead to an undesirable result. Since the
goal of his text is to present his opinion, the speaker takes responsibility for
his own assertions. Consequently, the source of modal expressions and rec-
ommendations is the speaker rather than some ostensibly agreed-on values
or axioms.

Thus, an apparently puzzling aspect of Havel's texts becomes meaningful
when viewed in the context of Czech politics and history. Havel's texts can
even be viewed as responding to the texts of professional politicians beyond
the Czech context. These observations suggest that a text requires consideration of a long cultural-historical-social memory on which it may be constructed and a comparative perspective to see how the text may interact with
contemporary and possibly future texts in the same genre.

Teaching Reading and Use of Technology for Less Commonly Taught Languages: Czech as an Example

The examples from three different languages given above demonstrate
that text interpretation requires analysis on two levels: micro-level properties
and macro-level properties. Parsing of the morphosyntactic function of each
word and the relations between clauses within a sentence belong to the
former, analysis of the interaction between sentence-level properties and
discourse to the latter. Discourse includes identifying referents, analyzing the
relations among sentences and paragraphs, and most important, analyzing
the speech situation: who is speaking to whom on what type of occasion and
with what type of cultural, social and historical assumptions. As shown in the
analysis of Mori's speeches, a cross-linguistic approach also helps sharpen
our understanding of a text. The final interpretation of forms and lexicon
largely depends on these parameters. As shown above, reading a text solely on
the micro level may yield potentially misguided interpretations unless accompanied by a reading on the macro level.

This issue is connected with the question of how a language teacher could
effectively use the increasingly accessible authentic materials on the Web. The

analysis of texts above suggests that assigning a text from the Web merely because it is authentic and teaching students how to parse it does not automatically constitute reading of a text or understanding culture. Besides, most authentic texts that are intellectually stimulating for college students, such as news, articles on culture, and anecdotes, are not easily accessible to beginning students of less commonly taught languages such as Czech; the language requires a relatively large amount of time to master the basic mechanics of grammar and a bulk of vocabulary that does not have many cognates in English. Clearly, some type of materials are needed to serve as a bridge between the student and authentic reading matter.

Electronic Reading Materials for Students of Multiple Levels

For Czech, materials that help students read independently have traditionally appeared as readers in a textbook format to be used above the first-year level (for example, Heim et al. 1985). For languages such as Czech, however, technology gives the Web much greater potential than the textbook format. One advantage of the Web is the relative ease with which materials may be updated. Publishers are usually reluctant to make changes in a textbook unless there is a high demand for it in the market. It also takes time to incorporate such changes into a textbook. On the Web, errors can be corrected, vocabulary can be adjusted, and new materials can be added immediately as the need arises at a relatively low cost.

The strength of Web technology, however, goes beyond such commercial considerations. Its nested structure allows readers to access grammar information and definitions of vocabulary terms *in context* while following the storyline (Duffelmeyer 1984, p. 513); this feature frees up time for reading in context and discussion of culture in the classroom. Unlike books, which tend to be cluttered with footnotes, Web sites have annotations that are hidden and do not distract the reader away from macro-level reading.

The HTML text also aids reading on both micro and macro levels for students at various stages of language learning. In a paper format there is no satisfactory way of creating multilevel material. Take, for example, the basic issue of providing vocabulary commentaries: a short vocabulary list or abbreviated grammar commentary makes the material less accessible to beginners, whereas extensive annotations are psychologically intimidating for them. Text on the Web can be in principle linked to as many vocabulary glosses as needed for various groups of readers, enabling them to choose only the type of information they need. Efficient and large-scale language input, especially exposure to language in *context* accompanied by many helping hands in parsing and vocabulary, accelerates the reading process, thereby allowing the instructor to introduce more advanced activities fairly early.

Furthermore, the text linked to the Web offers students an increasing sense of contact with the outside world. Classroom teaching alone often limits students to imaginary or artificial situations. Even with the presence of props and other materials, the classroom is somewhat detached from the culture and people being studied. Information in the book format tends to be quickly outdated. In contrast, if a text is linked to well-maintained Web sites, students can easily access the most current information about various aspects of Czech culture. Given specific tasks and specific sites that are appropriate for their levels, students with various academic interests can explore information actively. Intermediate- and advanced-level students will soon discover that Web pages in English do not offer as much information about Czech culture and realia as do those in Czech. If they are given carefully selected assignments, students will find reading in Czech more "real" and realize that certain types of information cannot be obtained without reading in the target language. Discovery of new sites related to individual interests keeps everyone excited about the country and about language learning and leads to active discussion in the classroom.

Basic Components of Czech Reading Materials

With respect to specific problems in teaching Czech, there are several components that may need to be included in materials on the Web. They are being studied in our *Comenius Web,* an ongoing project that currently exists as "Brown On-Line Czech Anthology" ⟨http://www.language.brown.edu/CZH/⟩. One preliminary component that may be self-evident but nonetheless significant is a section in English that discusses reading strategies for students and instructors. The traditional approach to reading in Czech has been based on parsing of individual sentences; the issue of combining both micro- and macro-level reading has not been extensively addressed by instructors of Czech. Students who are in the process of learning inflectional patterns tend to focus on the structural aspects of the language, and they are likely to need instructions on how micro- and macro-level reading strategies should mesh when they read a text.

Several other features may be incorporated to help accelerate students' rate of learning and reading on the micro level. Glossing of a text—parsing both grammar and vocabulary—helps students at different levels deal with the mechanics of individual sentences. Students at different levels of learning will benefit from two types of vocabulary explanation: English translation of the item and a Czech paraphrase. Retention of sentence patterns, grammatical properties, and lexicon can be enhanced by several other features: vocabulary entries listing both the English equivalent and Czech paraphrase, sound files for vocabulary entries and the text, paraphrasing exercises for stylistically marked lexical items, exercises in which students search for lexical items related to a specific theme, and grammar exercises that are related in content to the text. These exercises help increase knowledge of and structure of the lexicon and help students become readers of new texts who are careful with details.

Besides these features, which address micro-level reading, macro-level components are indispensable. Attention to this level starts with selection of texts. If the goal of reading is to incorporate macro-level components that are maximally useful for reading other texts, teaching materials should reflect the cultural "canon" in a language, representative texts that are known to an educated native speaker. These texts tend to recur and are recycled not only in literature but also in journalistic and political writings. The knowledge of such texts assists students in grasping the author's perspective and in understanding historical and cultural association that the author wishes to invoke in new texts.

Reading material located on the Web has great potential for incorporation of macro-level reading components. Links to the broader cultural context (for example, skimming for gist, hypothesis testing, summarization) can be placed in several parts of the text to allow beginning students to grasp the main flow of discourse. These exercises help develop the habit of engaging with the text, enabling students to contrast their expectations with the content of the text.

Links to information about the author, the text itself, and cultural annotations to the text, including its social and historical context and how it is being received by the current native audience, not only acquaint students with the general nature of the text but also help students learn the insiders' view of it. The latter leads to discussions of differences between students' interpretations and naive interpretations and also of changing interpretations by native readers over time. These discussions can be combined with exercises aimed at building salient, pragmatically and culturally appropriate discourse.

The links, which may be connected further to existing pages on the Web, may also be structured so that students of different language competencies can access different links to varying depths. Here, however, great care must be taken to insure that the tasks are specified for particular levels and that they are meaningful in terms of learning culture. For students who wish to pursue their academic interest in Czech language and culture, the Web is also capable of incorporating bibliographies and publications sites where students contribute their own papers in Czech studies; electronic mentoring would also be possible with Czech scholars who are scattered throughout the world.

Conclusions

In this chapter I have used speeches by three political leaders to show the significance of both micro- and macro-level aspects of text interpretation. In fact, the latter is crucial for understanding the functions of the former. Misreading of texts may lead to misunderstandings that may have practical and serious repercussions. I have also pointed out how materials on the Web that combine both aspects could benefit learning of reading in less commonly taught languages such as Czech that require a relatively large amount of time to reach proficiency. These materials will serve as a bridge between the student and the authentic materials that are becoming increasing available on the Web. They could accelerate the development of reading abilities of students at both the micro and the macro level and enhance the nature of classroom interactions.

Sources

William J. Clinton, State of the Union Address (January 27, 2000) http://www.washingtonpost.com/wpsrv/politics/special/states/docs/sou00.htm
Václav Havel, New Year's Addresses (January 1, 1994, 1995, 1997, 1998, 1999, 2000) http://www.hrad.cz/president/Havel/speeches/
Yoshiro Mori, Policy Speech to the 147th Session of the Diet (April 7, 2000) http://www.kantei.go.jp/jp/souri/2000/0407syosin.html
Yoshiro Mori, Policy Speech to the 149th Session of the Diet (July 28, 2000) http://www.kantei.go.jp/jp/souri/2000/0728syosin.html

References

Brown, P., and S. C. Levinson. (1987). *Politeness: Some Universals in Language Use.* Cambridge: Cambridge University Press.
Chung, S., and A. Timberlake. (1990). Tense, Aspect, and Mood. In *Language Typology and Syntactic Description,* edited by T. Shopen, pp. 202–58. Cambridge: Cambridge University Press.
Duffelmeyer, F. A. (1984). The Effect of Context Clues on the Vocabulary Test

Performance of Word Dominant and Paragraph Dominant Readers. *Journal of Reading* 27: 508–13.

Fairclough, N. (1989). *Language and Power.* London: Longman.

Givon, T. (1979). *On Understanding Grammar.* New York: Academic.

Havel, V. (1965). *Vyrozumění: Hra o 12 obrazech.* Prague: Dilia.

Heim, M., D. Worth, and Z. Meyerstein, eds. (1985). *Readings in Czech.* Columbus, Oh.: Slavica.

7

Experiential Learning and Collaborative Reading: Literacy in the Space of Virtual Encounters

SILKE VON DER EMDE AND JEFFREY SCHNEIDER

> *We induce (and seduce–perhaps even produce) the reader to join with us in shapeful behavior, recognizing emerging contour within the disclosures of the text. The contour is the figure of changing change, or how meaning is made.*
> —Michael Joyce, "MOO or Mistakenness"

It is likely no mere accident that innovations in educational technologies have contributed significantly to the renewed interest in the category of literacy in foreign language teaching and research. Although developing reading and writing skills has always been a hallmark of the foreign language curriculum at colleges and universities, the concept of literacy offers a new framework for thinking about reading and writing as intellectually rich processes that extend beyond skills development. At the same time, computer-assisted language learning (CALL) and, in particular, network-based language teaching (NBLT)—where "human-to-human communication is the focus" (Warschauer and Kern 2000, p. 1)—have greatly expanded what literacy means in a globalized information age in which reading and writing—even communication itself—are increasingly mediated by computers. Richard Kern, for instance, notes that computers not only "affect how we read" (Kern 2000, p. 233) but, when used in the classroom, also add "layers of complexity to an already complex process" (ibid., 224). This dual complexity—of literacy itself as well as of integrating technology into the language learning process—suggests new, dynamic possibilities for reconceiving the role of reading in the early sequences in the foreign language curriculum. Indeed, the focus on literacy reflects a growing consensus that skills-based, proficiency-oriented pedagogies have proved insufficient in preparing students to make the transition from lower-level "language" courses to upper-level "content" courses. Upper-level courses treat reading and writing not only as integral practices for developing students' critical thinking skills but also as primary tools for the production and dissemination of knowledge. Thus, realizing a literacy-oriented approach to foreign language learning requires that we introduce into elementary and intermediate courses the more complex theories and practices of reading featured in upper-level literary and cultural studies seminars.[1]

The move to literacy in second language acquisition (SLA) research has been instrumental in shifting the goals of intermediate foreign language reading practices away from comprehension, information retrieval, or skills development in the area of grammar and vocabulary to a new set of meaningful interactions with text. Swaffar, Arens, and Byrnes (1991), for instance, call for an end to "sentence-level" reading instruction that inevitably encourages simplistic "surface translation behavior" (p. 29) on the part of students. Instead, they appeal for literacy standards that recognize foreign language reading as an interactive and creative process that contributes to overall foreign language learning but at the same time is not limited by the student's proficiency in the foreign language (p. 53). Kern's concept of "active literacy" moves beyond a notion of normative literacy standards to define reading and writing as "an apprenticeship in new social practices—an encounter with new values, norms, and world views" (Kern 1998, p. 78). Though these models offer more dynamic conceptualizations of reading than older structuralist and cognitive approaches, they inevitably limit the full range of possible encounters with complex texts. All calls for literacy standards or "apprenticeship" implicitly run the risk of leaving the target culture intact as a stable, unitary reference point or assigning to reading the task of completing the circuit of communication with an idealized native speaker. Overall, the SLA-based literacy movement seems to tie interactions with literary and nonliterary texts too systematically to native-speaker-measured proficiency or functional knowledge about the target culture. From the perspective of literary and cultural studies, reading still comes up short in these models.

Thus, despite these important and expansive developments in foreign language reading practices, there has been little attempt to integrate more deconstructive and potentially liberating theories of reading from the fields of literary theory and cultural studies. Because literary and cultural studies have changed over time and fractured into particular theoretical camps that often have national characteristics—such as (German) aesthetics of reception, (French) structuralism and poststructuralism, and (Anglo-American) reader-response criticism—and competing claims, it is difficult to enclose the field within a unified historical narrative. Nevertheless, philosophers, literary critics, and cultural studies scholars are unified in raising fundamental and unsettling questions about all three entities involved in the reading process— the author, the text, and the reader: What constitutes authorship? What is a text? How do texts mean? What is the role of the reader in actualizing the meaning of a text? How does the very structure of language as a system of signs both expand and constrain interpretation? (For a helpful overview, see Eagleton 1983 and Calinescu 1993.) Far from reaching any final conclusions, theorists reject strictly communicative notions of reading and, instead, emphasize that reading is an open-ended and creative process involving essentially indeterminate texts. Rather than leading to a definitive understanding or comprehension of a "pre authored" and authoritative text, such notions stress that meaning is created, first and foremost, in the process of reading, or, to say it another way, it is the reader, not the author, who "constructs" the text under perusal. In fact, in postmodernist theories of reading the boundaries between reading and writing become blurred. As Matei Calinescu, following Roland Barthes, suggests, "creative *reading*—deep, meditative reading—is after all a recognizable form of 'production'" (1993, p. 140).

These kinds of insights have led a few SLA theorists, most prominently Claire Kramsch, to argue for a different model of reading in the foreign language classroom. Claire Kramsch's and Thomas Nolden's concept of "oppositional reading," for instance, describes how fourth-semester students can construct the text they are reading and thereby question its authority (Kramsch and Nolden 1994). The radical potential for foreign language reading emerges even more clearly in Kramsch's notion of "the privilege of the non-native speaker" (Kramsch 1997). By exposing the native speaker as a class-based "fiction" that obfuscates real tensions within any language community, Kramsch problematizes comprehension as an objective criterion for teaching and assessing reading and suggests instead that notions of pleasure and self-actualization might be more important objectives for foreign language reading—and language study more generally. Altogether, these new initiatives regarding reading and literacy not only seek to reframe foreign language learning as part of the larger intellectual mission of higher education in this country but also work to enfranchise learners who have tradi-

tionally been most disempowered by their linguistic skills and their un-
familiarity with the target culture.

Admittedly, such decentering notions of reading can easily overwhelm
language learners, who find the meaning of foreign language texts already too
indeterminate on the basis of their limited language skills. But, as Kramsch's
concept of the privilege of the nonnative speaker foregrounds, the very linguistic distance from a text can prove a boon as much as a hindrance. Thus,
although it is important to recognize that some degrees of comprehension
are not only possible but necessary and even desirable to promote exchange
and understanding between persons of different cultures and different languages, we may do our students a disservice when we confine elementary and
intermediate foreign language reading to comprehension or communication. If reading texts of a foreign culture primarily means learning the discourse conventions of that culture in order to facilitate smooth communication among speakers of different cultures, as even the new Focus on Form
movement has tended to suggest (see Doughty and Williams 1998; Lee and
Valdman 2000), we stop short of giving our students the opportunity to
explore the creative tensions between "the textual and the social" (Kramsch,
A'Ness, and Lam 2000). And we miss the opportunity of allowing our students to experiment with notions of authorship, fictionalization, and representation—the very concepts that enable them to engage critically with the
target culture as well as their native culture and thereby to realize the larger,
self-reflective goals laid out by higher education. Thus, it is critical that we
not define the textual and the social in relatively flat terms, whereby the
textual seems entirely authorized and constrained by the social context in
which it is *produced*. By placing, among other things, equal emphasis on the
real and possible contexts and conditions in which such texts are *received* as
well as produced (including the language classroom itself), literary and cultural studies inevitably open up richer interpretive tensions, even for foreign
language learners. After all, the differences among pluralistic and competing
social contexts—whether they be defined as linguistic communities, time
periods, or class- or gender-based groups, for example—should prevent any
simple binaristic notion of the text-social or the text-context relationship.

In this chapter we outline a model for introducing low-intermediate language learners to the complex modes of reading practiced in literary and
cultural studies. In addition to drawing on our training in these fields, this
model has emerged from our intensive classroom work with a German-
language MOO ("MOOssiggang") over the past few years and our efforts to
reflect critically on the role of technology in the foreign language classroom.[2]

A MOO (*m*ulti-user domain, *o*bject *o*riented) is an on-line text-mediated virtual-reality space, where multiple users interact and communicate in a "room" and can move from "room" to "room." Evolved from the *Dungeons and Dragons* game software in the 1970s, the MOO has become what Kern calls one of the "most novel environments for social interaction and collaborative learning on the Internet" (Kern 1998, p. 76). Elsewhere we have explained general uses for MOOs in the language classroom, including how we have used it to collaborate with native speakers at the University of Münster in Germany (von der Emde, Schneider, and Kötter 2001) and to transform the low-intermediate language class into a cultural studies seminar (Schneider and von der Emde 2000). In this essay, however, we would like to focus on how the MOO recasts foreign language reading as a collaborative, experiential, and circular enterprise. As Warschauer and Kern suggest, "new technologies do not only *serve* the new teaching/learning paradigms, they also help *shape* [them]" (2000, p. 12). Thus, though this application of the MOO draws on important general principles of language learning pedagogy as well as reading practices in literary studies, the result was less a series of discrete units focused on reading than a semester-long approach that reshaped the classroom into a *literacy community* in which reading became writing, writing became reading, and students began to create a German language virtual culture that helped them reflect on the very process of reading from their privileged position as foreign language readers. The readings in this third-semester German course consisted of primary documents from the first half of the twentieth century, including film excerpts, maps, and short, thematic passages in German ranging from literary texts by Franz Kafka, Irmgard Keun, and Else Lasker-Schüler to political and autobiographical texts by Oswald Spengler, Thomas Mann, and Rosa Luxemburg. The verbal and visual texts were organized into general thematic units devoted to space and identity and offered exposure to a particularly important historical moment in German culture. We also sought to provide a series of collaborative and experiential activities to help students become informed, independent readers capable of sustained reflection on the reading process. To this end, we drew on our increasingly expanding sense of what is possible in a MOO: not only its capacity for synchronous computer-mediated communication (CMC) but also the rich asynchronous forms of writing in a MOO, which open up powerful opportunities for reflecting on the process of reading itself as a creative and playful process of (re)writing. As we shall point out, the important spatial dimensions of the MOO allow for a unique circular and circling visualization of the reading process itself: a sense of literacy in the space of virtual encounters.

Collaborative Reading

The MOO is an inherently collaborative space that radically expands the possibilities for language learning. On the most obvious level, the synchronous, text-based form of discussion in the MOO allows students to work together in small groups with their classmates or in teams consisting of native speakers or language learners at other colleges and universities. As studies of CMC have shown, the on-line discussion format offers many advantages over traditional face-to-face discussions: it reduces negative affective filters that often accompany oral performance in the classroom, it dramatically increases target language use and class participation, and it enables more sophisticated language use (see Beauvois 1992, 1994, 1997; Kern 1995). Yet communicating in the MOO does more than facilitate classroom discussions in another medium. We want to suggest that the intensely student-centered format of on-line group work initiates students into a process we call collaborative reading, in which the very act of reading—of actualizing the text—is the result of teamwork and dialogic engagement with the text. This is not to say that students do not develop their own individual interpretations—they do that, too—but they begin to realize that reading is a social act as much as it is a personal relationship with the text. As Kern explains, "A literacy-based orientation to language teaching . . . means engaging learners in reading and writing as acts of communication," which leads students to "become aware of the complex webs, rather than isolated strands, of meaning in human communication" (Kern 2000, pp. 45–46). In the case of our classroom work in the MOO, students used on-line discussions to collaborate on actualizing texts. Since they worked among themselves with only suggestive, optional questions from us as additional guidance, they also had the opportunity to playfully experiment with ideas and try out different readings of the text with their peers in ways that generally exceed group work in a traditional classroom.

This collaborative reading practice facilitated basic language learning at the level of vocabulary development. But more important, it also promoted richer, more contextualized forms of language learning, which resulted from developing interpretations of texts within the act of communicating with fellow learners. For instance, several important facets of collaborative reading emerge in the following discussion of a short excerpt by Thomas Mann titled "Im Spiegel" (In the Mirror), an autobiographical text solicited for a magazine in 1907:

CLIFFK sagt, "er spricht auch ueber seine Schule"
MARIEL sagt, "und er hatte ein schimpfliche Vergangenheit"

PORTIAS sagt, "aber Cliff hast du mir nicht erzahlt, dass er Schwul war?"

CLIFFK sagt, "hmm . . . was heisst Schwul?"

PORTIAS sagt, "gay"

CLIFFK sagt, "ahh . . . das war nicht mich"

PORTIAS sagt, "also, aber ist er?"

CLIFFK sagt, "Ich vergesse, wer das gesagt hat"

CLIFFK sagt, "ich weiss gar nicht"

CLIFFK sagt, "Irgendwer hat gesagt, dass Hintergrundtext 1 das gesagt hat"

PORTIAS sagt, "naja, es is nur interessant das er so viel ueber seine Frau spricht"

CLIFFK sagt, "Ja, stimmt . . . es ist interressant"

PORTIAS sagt, "es ist wie er versucht immer noch sich zu beweisen"

PORTIAS sagt, "weist du?"

PORTIAS sagt, "was denkt darueber Marie?"

PORTIAS sagt, "denkst*"

MARIEL sagt, "War 'Im Spiegel' in einen Zeitschrift? Dann er wollte Leute zu einen 'normal' Familie sehen."

PORTIAS sagt, "ja, genau"

CLIFFK sagt, "das ist moeglich"

PORTIAS sagt, "aber er wiederspricht ihm selbst, finde ich"

MARIEL sagt, "Er spricht ueber seinen Gluecke. Ist das sarkastisch?"

CLIFFK sagt, "hmm . . . ich glaube nicht"

PORTIAS sagt, "ja, ich auch nicht"

CLIFFK sagt, "Er schrieb ueber eine schoene Frau und Kinder"

CLIFFK sagt, "und sein Komfort; herrlichsten Moebeln, Teppichen und Kunstgemaelden"

PORTIAS sagt, "hmmm"

MARIEL sagt, "Ist er nicht in einen Gosse? Mit einen Frau, obwohl er ist Schwul?"

PORTIAS sagt, "er ist ganz Stolz"

CLIFFK says, "he's also speaking about his school"

MARIEL says, "and he had a disgraceful past"

PORTIAS says, "but, Cliff, didn't you tell me he was gay (schwul)?"

CLIFFK says, "hmm . . . what does 'Schwul' mean?"

PORTIAS says, "gay"

CLIFFK says, "ahh . . . that wasn't me"

PORTIAS says, "okay, but is he?"

CLIFFK says, "I forget who said that"

CLIFFK says, "I don't know"

CLIFFK says, "Someone said that the first background text said that"

PORTIAS says, "okay, but it is just interesting that he speaks so much about his wife"

CLIFFK says, "yeah, right . . . it is interesting"

PORTIAS says, "it's as if he's still trying to prove himself"

PORTIAS says, "you know?"

PORTIAS says, "what do you thinks (denkt) about it, Marie?"

PORTIAS says, "think* (denkst)"

MARIEL says, "Was 'In the Mirror' (Im Spiegel) in a magazine? Then he wanted people to see a 'normal' family."

PORTIAS says, "yes, exactly"

CLIFFK says, "that's possible"

PORTIAS says, "but he contradicts himself, I think"

MARIEL says, "He talks about his happiness (Glueck). Is that sarcastic?"

CLIFFK says, "hmm . . . I don't think so"

PORTIAS says, "yes, I also don't think so"

CLIFFK says, "He wrote about his beautiful wife and children"

CLIFFK says, "and his comfort; marvellous furniture, carpets and paintings"

PORTIAS says, "hmmm"

MARIEL says, "But isn't he in a gutter (Gosse)? With a wife, although he is gay?"

PORTIAS says, "he is quite proud"

(Note: This and the following reproduced transcripts are excerpts from logs made of student discussions in the MOO. All typographical and other errors are original to the text. All students are cited throughout by pseudonyms.)

In approaching this short but difficult text, the students demonstrate some basic reading skills that are critical to understanding the text: they return regularly to the words in the text (*schimpfliche Vergangenheit, schöne Frau, Komfort, Gosse,* for instance), they account for the genre of the text and make inferences about its intended audience, and they activate the contextual knowledge about the text and author contained in English-language background materials (the *Hintergrundtexte*) we made available in the MOO.[3] In their call for teaching "critical competence" rather than merely "communicative competence" in the intermediate language classroom, Jörg Roche and Mark Webber argue that "instruction must give students the possibility to work on complex topics even with their limited linguistic means of expression" (1995, p. 14). It is our experience that even in the face of periodic frustration at trying to convey complex thoughts about difficult texts in German, most students enjoy the challenge and even feel liberated and motivated by the focus on ideas. Despite their own grammatical problems in this written "oral discourse," the students generally understand each other, as evidenced in their responses: "ja, genau" (yes, exactly), "das ist moeglich" (that's possible), and "ich glaube nicht" (I don't think so). When communication problems do arise, they give each other important feedback (Cliff's request for the meaning of the word *schwul,* for example). More important, however, the discussion demonstrates that all three students have a basic understanding of the text, in which Thomas Mann discusses his attainment of an ideal bourgeois existence—a beautiful wife, a comfortable home, and professional success—in light of his dismal performance as a student and his teachers' dire predictions for his future.

Although the students exhibit good comprehension at the sentence level, they nevertheless raise important questions—and even disagree—about what the text *means.* Portia, for instance, wonders why Thomas Mann writes so much about his wife if he is supposed to be gay. Marie and Cliff disagree about whether Thomas Mann is actually happy in his bourgeois married existence. As all three realize, the two questions are intimately related and form the crux of their collaborative attempt to actualize the text for themselves. And the results are rather impressive. Although Cliff is quite content to take Mann's word choice at face value, Marie provides the key insight into vocabulary when she realizes that words such as *schimpfliche Vergangenheit* (disgraceful past) are less important for what they mean literally than for how they signify irony and sarcasm. Portia's focus on Mann's reputed homosexuality also seems to lead to an understanding of the dissimulation required for a married homosexual who might need to compensate for this "deficit" publicly—as Portia says, "sich beweisen" (to prove oneself). Marie connects the text's publication with Mann's public play with a private secret: "Dann er wollte Leute zu einen 'normal' Familie sehen" (Then he wanted people to see a "normal" family). At several points in the discussion, each effort to develop an interpretation—first Portia's and then Marie's—encounters resistance, in the form of either disagreement or missing enthusiasm from the others. But such resistance only spurs on the proponents to clarify their points and convince their partners. In the end, Marie's conclusion—that Mann's marriage represents the real unhappy "Gosse" (gutter) to which Mann's bad grades were supposed to lead him—represents a sophisticated and immensely satisfying reading. At one level, Marie's interpretation cannot be seen in terms of communication or some notion of comprehension, since it can never be traced conclusively back to the author's intentions and, in fact, might even be rejected by Mann himself. On another level, Marie's use of Mann's word "Gosse" in her counterreading represents the type of textual production that Barthes advocates, since she is in fact rewriting Mann's text by using his original words to actualize her own reading of the passage. That move adds an entirely new layer of irony on top of Mann's own.

Collaborative reading experiences like this one point toward the possibility of using reading to reorganize language learning itself. In this example, it gives someone like Marie, whose linguistic skills are much weaker than those of her two partners, not only a chance to contribute equally in the class but also a chance to reap self-actualizing, intellectual rewards in the very process of learning the language. The reconceptualization of reading within a collaborative framework shifted the value of language learning for other students in the class, too, even for something as fundamental as vocabulary building. For instance, in one of the regular self-evaluations that students completed in English at the end of each unit, one student, Daniel, acknowledged for himself the importance of vocabulary development for engaging with the complex texts we were reading: "Through readings of the authors like Rosa Luxemburg and Franz Kafka, it became lucid at least to myself that I lacked a decent amount of vocabulary needed to understand their works." But he went on to reframe the issue of vocabulary within the moment of collaboration with his fellow students, when, he wrote, "I was looking for vocabulary: words and ideas that I wanted to express but couldn't because I lacked some important vocabulary. This process made me develop my goals of learning a larger vocabulary, especially on my own, and put emphasis on this part of my studies." This student's understanding of vocabulary in both situations is subtly but distinctly different. Daniel characterizes the vocabulary he was missing for the comprehension of the readings as a "decent amount," a matter of quantity, and the kind of vocabulary he needed to express his ideas about the texts to others as "important," a matter of quality. Although reading authentic German texts builds vocabulary as an integral part of language learning, it is the moment of collaborative interpretation that personalizes the significance of vocabulary as the very basis for participation in a literacy community—even if that community consists of other language learners rather than native speakers. Reading does not, of course, naturally help students build vocabulary. As Susanne Rott argues, "describing incidental vocabulary gain as a 'by-product' of reading really does not capture the range of cognitive processes involved in meaning assignment and word learning" (2000, p. 275). Her study, however, examines only individual students' local, global, and word-inferencing strategies through think-aloud processes and does not assess the potential impact students' reading rich, open texts in order to jointly interpret their meaning rather than merely comprehend them as information. As Daniel's reflection indicates, the motivation of students to learn vocabulary increases when the stakes of conveying ideas are high.

Experiential Reading

Synchronous discussions are not the only or the most interesting use of the MOO to promote literacy. Thus, rather than limit students to straightforward discussions of texts, images, and films from the first half of the twentieth century that we were using to study space and identity, we also devoted considerable time to working within the space of the MOO in other ways, including role plays and writing and reading activities that contribute directly to the expansion of MOOssiggang's German-language virtual culture. Over the course of the semester, for instance, several assignments asked students to produce and analyze virtual identities, notes, letters, rooms, and other objects. In the MOO, all objects consist essentially of text and hence provide excellent opportunities for writing and reading. Moreover, because the MOO is a public space and easily makes student texts available not only to teachers but also to fellow students, it expands the audience—and thus raises the stakes—for student writing. On a pedagogical-political level, this "creative" writing runs parallel to the creative texts they are reading and consequently builds a bridge between authors such as Kafka and Luxemburg and the foreign language learners who read them. Indeed, since student writing in the MOO is a form of cultural production itself, it answers Russell Berman's call to "envision a strategy designed to elicit active producers who engage in a culture rather than merely receive it" (Berman 1994, p. 10). As Claire Kramsch and Thomas Nolden have pointed out, however, this engagement only occurs when students have the opportunity to value their own writing by subjecting it to the same kinds of cultural analyses that are practiced in the classroom on published writing by native speakers (Kramsch and Nolden 1994). Interpreting student writing in the MOO differs in quality from engagement with other forms of disseminated student writing, including writing on the Web. As Michael Joyce argues, MOO rooms and their objects have an experiential dimension to them that opens up the realm of reading. Because asynchronous writing in the MOO becomes the setting for synchronous communication, texts such as "rooms mean to be both the expression and occasion of their interactions. The room is what you read and where you write (sometimes writing what you read and where you write the next time)" (Joyce 2000, p. 42). Although Joyce is referring explicitly to room descriptions, his overall argument about the fundamental interaction between synchronous and asynchronous forms of writing in the MOO is more complex, since his point refuses any simple or stable distinction between these forms of writing or, for that matter, between reading and writing. The theoretical leverage of erasing those distinctions foregrounds the rich experiential dimension of reading and interacting in the MOO. Thus, if the MOO encourages a "readerly writing," then it also calls for "writerly reading" practices, something we sought to emphasize in the next series of activities.

Creating personal rooms in the MOO was one of the first writing assignments in the semester and came after students had read only a few texts. But once the rooms were completed, they became the occasion for several kinds of experiential reading assignments. Although some rooms seem more expansive and elaborate than others, it is possible to demonstrate the experiential nature of MOO writing and reading with a fairly short and straightforward one, such as Nora's room, which we actually used as our main example in a class session devoted to reflecting on the informal encounters students had when they initially visited each other's rooms. Nora's room contains a graphic of the band Radiohead followed by this text:

> Noras Zimmer ist ein wundervoll Platzt. In diesem Zimmer spielt die Band Radiohead immer. Nicht die CDs, aber DIE BAND!!! Nora hat ihnen entfuert, so sie muessen nur fuer Nora spielen. Alle von Radioheads Musikausruestung liegt in diesem Zimmer. Nun kann jeden Tag ein tolles Musikkonzert sein! Die Zimmer ist eine kliene blaue Raum mit einem Bett, einem Computer, keiner Stereoanlage (wer brauch eine Stereo, wenn man hat Radiohead?), und vielen Sofas fuer nur gute/n Freundinen und Freunden.

> (Nora's room is a wonderful place. In this room, the band Radiohead is always playing. Not the CD's, but THE BAND!!!! Nora has kidnapped them, so they have to play only for her. All of Radiohead's music equipment is lying in this room. Now there can be a great concert every day! The room is a small blue room with a bed, a computer, no stereo system (who needs a stereo, when you have Radiohead?), and many sofas for only good friends.)

Of course, though we work with students on developing basic writing skills, we used this example to focus on student writing as an opportunity for reading. Nora's room description contains some grammatical errors, but her fellow students had little problem comprehending the text. And although the description may strike some as a little naïve, it actually provoked a range of responses in our class discussion. For instance, one student observed that only close friends seem to be welcome here and that there is not any space for others. This student, who did not know Nora very well, felt left out. We also discussed how Nora's explicit insistence that she and her friends are hearing live (rather than recorded) music from her favorite band uses the on-line environment to express a wish for presence and authentic experience that would surpass some of the experiences in her CD-mediated world.

In addition to this general class discussion focused on reading, we used two activities—one explicitly collaborative and one of a more formal nature—to structure and extend the experiential reading opportunities afforded by these student texts in the MOO. In the collaborative assignment, we asked students to respond to each other's rooms by creating a house-warming gift and explaining it in a letter to the room's owner in terms of the room. Nora's room, for instance, elicited the following texts from Daniel:

Geschenk fuer Nora. Mein Geschenk fuer Nora ist eine Buehne fuer Radiohead. Ich gebe sie diese Geschenk, denn sie die Gruppre Radiohead in ihrem
Zimmer hat. Aber wo wird die Gruppe spielen? Jetzt kann die Gruppe an der
Buehne spielen. Jetzt geht es sehr gut bei der Gruppe und Radiohead wird
gluecklich sein. Die Gruppe wird besser spielen, wenn sie sehr gluecklich mit
dem Zimmer ist. Ob die Personnen von Radiohead gluecklich sind, werden
sie nie den Beruf verlassen.

(My gift for Nora is a stage for Radiohead. I am giving her this gift because
she has the group Radiohead in her room. But where will the group play?
Now the group can play on her stage. Now it will be very good for the group,
and Radiohead will be happy. The group will play better if they are happy
with the room. Whether [sic] the persons of Radiohead are happy, they will
never leave their career.)

Liebe Nora, ich habe dein Zimmer sehr gern. Ich will dass du Radiohead auch
gern hat. Ich habe gern das Quotation "Es ist leicht ungluecklich zu sein, aber
es ist besser gluecklich zu sein." Es ist von einem Lied. Ich finde es toll, dass
Radiohead live in deinem Zimmer spielen. Ich mochte in deinem Zimmer
immer sein! Vielleicht kann ich an deinem Sofas in deim Raum sein. Aber
ich denke, dass su ein Stereo noch haben musst. Andere Gruppen sind auch
sehr gut. So macht Spass mit deiner Gruppe Radiohead in deinem Zimmer.
—Daniel

(Dear Nora, I like your room a lot. I want you to like Radiohead very much. I
like the quotation "It is easy to be unhappy, but better to be happy." It is from
a song. I think it's great that Radiohead plays live in your room. I would like
to always be in your room! Perhaps I can be at your sofas in the room. But I
think that you also have to have a stereo still. Other groups are also very good.
So, have fun with your group Radiohead in your room!—Daniel)

Daniel's gift and letter represent a reading of the room that engages with
Nora's text on several levels. On one level, it affirms the value of the space she
created by providing an object designed to secure its meaning and existence,
since, as Daniel theorizes, if the players feel comfortable, they will not only
play better but also want to stay in Nora's room. On a second level, however,
his gift also engages critically with Nora's text. Rather than succumbing to her
fantasy of presence and self-indulgence in the music, Daniel's reasons for the
stage gently push Nora to think beyond her own pleasures and take her inhab-
itants' comfort into account. In a sense, Daniel is suggesting that Nora's wish
for presence and intimacy with others in the MOO (including Radiohead)
must be carried through by a willingness to deal with the messy details of what

that presence implies: consideration and, potentially, accommodation of others and their needs. Finally, the sentence in his letter asking whether he can sit on her for-friends-only couch signals his amicable intentions by stressing the personal bond they share as fans of Radiohead. Although Daniel's texts are informal, indirect, and even implicit readings of Nora's room, they demonstrate that careful peer engagement with student writing can and should initiate new texts that themselves call for new readings.

For the formal assignment, students were expected to offer an explicit interpretation of a MOO room produced by a student at another college. Modeled on our class discussion of Nora's room, these interpretations focused not only on the content of the rooms but also on the ways that the texts constructed the reader and related to the discourse conventions of the MOO. Brady's experience of Stefan's room produced the following sophisticated reading, which refers explicitly to the experience of being in the space:

> Interpretation von Stefans Gruft. In seinem Zimmer erschaeft Stefan sehr wirksam eine dunkle, einschuechternde Laune. Seine Beschreibungen und der Gebrauch von Ansprache des Lesers macht das Zimmer sehr lebenswahr—man fuehlt, wie er echt in dem Zimmer steht. Das ist aber nicht unbedingt gut! Das Zimmer macht einen sehr aengstlich unruhig, es ist furchtbar geheimnisvoll. Die Name des Zimmers, Stefans Gruft, ist sehbst schrecklich, und der Rest des Texts folgt aehnlich. Anscheinend hat Stefan Lust, Leute zu erschrecken! Ich habe mich gewuendert, ob Stefan echt so dunkel wie sein Zimmer ist oder ob er das Zimmer als ein Witz gemacht hat. Die Beschreibung des Zimmers hoert sich sehr an, als ob es in 'Dungeons & Dragens' (ein Rollenspiel) pasen wuerde, so habe ich gedacht, dass vielleicht Stefan das gern hat. Dann muss er nicht echt selbst duester sein, aber darf er noch solche Sachen gern haben. Ich wuensche, dass ich Stefan im MOO sprechen koennte, weil ich mehr wissen will.

> (Interpretation of Stefan's Tomb. In his room Stefan very effectively creates a dark, intimidating mood. His description and use of addressing the reader makes the room very true-to-life—you feel like you are in a real room. But that is not necessarily good! The room makes you very afraid and uneasy; it is very mysterious. Even the name of the room, Stefan's *tomb*, is horrible, and the rest of the text follows similarly. Apparently, Stefan delights in scaring people! I wondered whether Stefan is really so dark as his room or whether he made the room as a joke. The description of the room sounds as if it would fit in "Dungeons & Dragons," so I thought that perhaps Stefan likes that. But then he himself doesn't have to be really dark and forbidding, but he may like such things. I wish that I could speak with Stefan in the MOO because I want to know more!)

Often, MOO room descriptions begin with the phrase "you see" as a strategy of inserting the reader into the text itself. Although typically this convention of addressing the reader underlines forms of community in the MOO, Brady notices in this case a kind of aggressive tone in Stefan's efforts to address the reader directly. Perhaps because of the imaginative setting of this and other student rooms in the MOO, Brady also recognizes that texts are not necessarily autobiographical and that readers need to be careful about inferring things about the author from the text in a direct way. She understands that authors can play with identity through language, particularly in the MOO, which, as she mentions, is an ideal environment for role-playing. Despite the formal nature of the assignment, however, Brady's interpretation does not signal the end of her engagement with the text. Rather than containing her encounter within her own written response, she instead expresses the wish to follow up her reading with a conversation with the author, who would not only supply her with feedback on her own impressions but also potentially answer other questions generated by Stefan's text. Because these interpretations were read by the room's owner (students placed them in the rooms they were interpreting) as well as by the instructors, such writerly readings, which of course are themselves texts, respond to the writer's invitation to "join in shapeful behavior" (Joyce's phrase) with an implicit invitation back to the author.

Indeed, Brady's desire for a conversation reminds us that synchronous communication in the MOO is experiential as well as collaborative. The MOO offers space to assume a new identity—whether by choosing a new name or gender or by living out a different personality (either an aspect of the user's own or an entirely new one that is marked by his or her real name). As Sherry Turkle suggests, the MOO—like the Internet more generally—"has become a significant social laboratory for experimenting with the constructions and reconstructions of self that characterize postmodern life. In its virtual reality, we self-fashion and self-create" (Turkle 1995, p. 180). We decided to tap the power of role-playing for enriching the reading experience and to examine the complex connection between identity and textual representation. We assigned students specific roles (either authors or characters from the texts we had read), which they were then asked to prepare ahead of time by rereading the appropriate text or texts. The fact that students did not know who was playing the other roles when they entered the MOO increased the authenticity of the experience. The assignment for the role play was to develop a concept for a German MOO museum devoted to the first half of the twentieth century. Thus, the students had to argue for their author or character from within that role, and they had to confront other authors and characters and their goals and intentions. Designed as an open-ended, task-based activity, the role play produced a variety of results, with some groups working out a solution and others failing to reach consensus. More important than the specific group results were the implications for reading, which, as Calinescu notes, is inherently performative in an analogous way to role-playing in the MOO:

> To read a literary work is to perform in several senses of the word. It is, first, to perform a role—the role of the reader as "scripted" in the text. . . . To read is, second, to perform in one's own mind the roles of major characters in a work of fiction—to become something of an actor who switches roles in an extended mental solo performance. But in a third sense, to read is also a kind of mental stage directing, which includes, aside from coaching the fictive actors, designing the sets, selecting the costumes, and visualizing such expressive details as gestures, movements, and faces. To read is, in other words, to give voice, articulation, and shape to the text's silent language, to fill out its "spots of indeterminacy" (Ingarden), to give meaning and life to the printed page in one's imagination. (1993, p. 275)

In a sense, then, the act of role-playing in the MOO rehearsed and even literalized—since role-playing in the MOO uses written dialogues—for the students the very dimensions of play present in any act of reading.

If reading is a form of performance, it is not surprising that acting it out in a role play with others who have read the same texts produced important insights for our students. In theories of experiential learning, however, experience is never sufficient to guarantee the full measure of learning, since, as Viljo Kohonen explains, "only experience that is reflected upon seriously will yield its full measure of learning" (Kohonen 1992, p. 17). Thus, we followed up the role play with an assignment asking students to reflect on the activity by reading their own role play log plus the logs of two other groups and discussing them in a subsequent session with the other members of their role play group. These follow-up discussions suggest that the experience of playing an author or character produced new insights into the texts as well as thoughtful reflections on reading:

> BARBARAM sagt, "ich habe die Autor/Innen von dieser Zeit mehr interessant gefunden"
> BARBARAM sagt, "Lucy, kannst du noch mal erklaeren, was du meinst? ich bin nicht sicher . . ."
> BARBARAM sagt, "meinst du Frauen?"
> ROBERTB sagt, "Ich habe gelernt, dass alle diese Leute traurire Leben haetten"
> LUCYK sagt, "Ich sagte dass Kafka homisexual war. Das meint nicht dass Freuen ihn verwirr."

BARBARAM sagt, "ja, Robert, du hast genau recht"

THOMASB sagt, "Ja, jetzt die autors gefallt mir besser."

THOMASB sagt, "Ich verstehe die Lebens der Autors besser."

LUCYK sagt, "ja"

BARBARAM sagt, "jetzt will ich auch etwas mehr von jeder lesen"

BARBARAM sagt, "es war schoen, dass wir alle uns gut vorbereiten haben . . ."

ROBERTB sagt, "das stimmt, Thomas"

THOMASB sagt, "Ja Barbara, ich bin einverstanden."

BARBARAM sagt, "damit haben wir die Moeglichkeit alle die Autor/Innen besser zu verstehen"

BARBARAM sagt, "es hat viel Spass gemacht"

(BARBARAM says, "I found the authors from this time period more interesting"

BARBARAM says "Lucy, can you explain again what you mean? I'm not sure (what you meant) . . ."

BARBARAM says, "do you mean women?"

ROBERTB says, "I learned that all these people had sad lives"

LUCYK says, "I said that Kafka was homosexual. That doesn't mean that women confused him"

BARBARAM says, "yes, Robert, you are exactly right"

THOMASB says, "Yes, now I like the authors more."

THOMASB says, "I understand the lives of the authors better."

LUCYK says, "yes"

BARBARAM says, "now I want to read more by each (author)"

BARBARAM says, "it was nice that we were all prepared well (for the role play) . . ."

ROBERTB says, "you're right, Thomas"

THOMASB says, "Yes, Barbara, I agree with you."

BARBARAM says, "thus we had the possibility to understand all the authors better"

BARBARAM says, "it was a lot of fun")

After the initial frustration that students often experienced in reading and discussing these difficult German primary texts the first time around in the semester, it is no surprise that they enthusiastically respond to what they perceive as unadulterated play in this activity: "es hat viel Spass gemacht" (it was a lot of fun). It is important that the dimension of fun in role-playing broke down the rigid dichotomy between work and play that often informs the experience of reading in college, especially in the lower levels of the foreign languages, when students tend to read more slowly and less confidently. But these students also testify that the activity of playing these authors and characters gave them new "knowledge" about the authors. Although Lucy's claim that Kafka was homosexual might be hotly debated and is most likely incorrect, more than anything else, it continues the class's earlier efforts to connect the enigmatic irony of Mann's text with his reputed homosexuality and signals her attempt to make sense of the enigmatic quality of Kafka's text in terms of her awareness of his problematic relationship with women. (These student attempts, of course, follow a long historical tradition. Eve Sedgwick [1990], for instance, has famously argued that textual and narrative secrets become linked to homosexuality in the nineteenth and twentieth centuries.) In distinction to Lucy's focus on Kafka, however, Barbara, Thomas, and Robert all refer to authors in the plural. Indeed, the insights into the role play seem to stem as much from the collaborative dimensions of the role play as from preparing and playing the specific individual roles, which, as Barbara concludes, was well done. The reference to authors in the plural suggests that the interaction between all the roles moved students' understanding from the specific texts they had reread in preparation for the role play to the *intertextual* connections that emerged through that interaction. Although Robert saw, and Barbara confirmed, a common sadness in their lives, the satisfaction of that insight—perhaps strengthened by the identification from assuming their roles—also increased their interest in reading more texts by all the authors.

Circular Reading

Whether through the dimensions of collaborative or experiential reading, our activities in the MOO encouraged students to return again and again to the course readings. The result was the students' growing awareness of the inexhaustibility of complex texts—as a result of the play of language or of the constant emergence of new intertextual contexts for understanding. Our final assignment of the semester sought once again to exploit the dynamic sense of space in the MOO, not only to induce students to return again to the text but also to help them reflect on reading and rereading as diachronic and synchronic processes. Modern theories of reading often assign the initial reading of a text a temporal dimension, while in rereading the expanded sense of a text assumes the spatial metaphors of landscape and architecture (Calinescu 1993, pp. 17–18). Although an absolute distinction does not hold up under scrutiny, "in the world of (re)reading, the chronological-historical flow of phenomenal time actually is reversed insofar as we recognize the essential circularity of citation" (ibid., p. 53). The MOO, which is organized on an architectural metaphor of rooms and exits, provides an excellent medium for exploring and representing such a circular experience of reading, especially since rooms can be connected to each other in ways that are not tied to a unidirectional (chronological) sense of time. The final activity of the course consisted of having students build exits from their rooms to five or more texts they had read in the course and then explain their choices in an essay that would also be available as a note in their room. Students were free to choose either student rooms (made by other Vassar students or by students at our partner college) or the individual rooms that the instructors had created for each author or topic. By linking their room to other rooms, students represented their own personal and intellectual relationships with other texts. But the activity also concretized for students the intertextual reading process by offering a visual representation through the architectural metaphor of the MOO. Indeed, it established a web of intertextuality across the entire class, since anyone in the MOO could follow a link to another room, which could then lead to additional texts and links in ways that might create circular patterns.

As the following student essay by Lucy demonstrates, the students' explanations of their exits to other rooms reveal a series of intertextual connections on a number of different intellectual and personal levels:

> Ich habe eine Auesgange zu Weltflucht gebaut, weil das Gedicht viele interessanten Ideen enthält. Ich mag Gedichten und denke dass es staunlich ist, wenn man alle Interpretationen hoeren. Als meine Gruppe in der MOO ueber das Gedicht spreochen hat, waren die Ideen von anderen Leute zu mir neu. Ich dachte, dass das Gedicht euber Alter und Tod sprecht, sondern andere Leute dachten, dass es sprecht, wie eine Gesellschaft eine Person ersticken kann.
>
> Ich habe eine Auesgange zu Noras Zimmer gemacht. Noras Zimmer sprecht ueber das Band Radiohead. Radiohead ist mein beliebtes Band und sie passen in dem Weimar Republik hinein, weil sie ueber Gesellschaft in den Liedern sprechen. Alle Autoren in dem Weimar Republik kritisieren Gesellschaft und Radiohead kritisert Technologie in eueren Gesellschaft.
>
> Ich habe ein Tunnel zu Kafka gemacht. Kafka ist ein wunderbarer Autor. In "Der Bau," hat er eine Metapher fuer sein Leben gemacht. Die Text wie ein Raetsel ist. Die Text ist spass zu lesen, weil Kafka die Bedeutung versteckt. Ich moechte mehr Kafka lesen. Wenn ich habe gelernt, dass Kafka die Maulwurf war, wollte ich mehr Kafka lesen.
>
> Ich habe Irmgard (Keun) fuer mein Rollenspiel gespielt, und ich denke jetzt, dass sie wichtig zu mir ist. Dies ist der Grund, warum ich eine Ausgaenge zu ihr gemacht habe. Vielleicht, weil sie nicht so bekannt wie Kafka, Mann, oder Lusemburg ist, ist es gut eine Auesgange zu Irmgard zu machen. Obwohl sie nicht so starke Meinungen wie Rosa Luxemburg hat, ist sie auch faszinierend.

Ich habe eine Ausgange zu Stefans Zimmer gebaut. Ich habe es inter-
pretiert und ihm ein Geschenk gegeben. Seine Autobiographie enthält viele
Einblicken in Leben, die mich uber meine Kindheit zu reflektieren veran-
lassen. Stefans Leben is dem Lebens der Autoren aehnlich. Stefan und die
Autoren haben in Laaendern mit politischen Unruhen gewohnt. Thomas
Mann, Irmgard Keun, und Rosa Luxemburg erlebten die Nazis, waehrend
Stefan eine kommunisitsche Regierung erlebte.

I built exits to "Weltflucht" ["World Flight" by Else Lasker-Schüler] because the poem contains many interesting ideas. I like poetry and think that it
is amazing when you hear all the different intepretations. When my group in
the MOO spoke about the poem, many of the ideas of other people were new
to me. I thought that the poem spoke about aging and death, but other
people thought that it spoke about how a society can suffocate a person.

I also made an exit to Nora's room. Nora's room talks about the band
Radiohead. Radiohead is my favorite band and they fit in with the Weimar
Republic because they talk about society in their songs. All the authors in the
Weimar Republic criticize society and Radiohead criticizes technology in
your society.

I also made a tunnel to Kakfa['s room]. Kafka is a wonderful author. In
"Der Bau" ["The Burrow"] he made a metaphor for his life. The text is like a
riddle. The text is fun to read because Kafka hid the meaning. I would like to
read more Kafka. When I learned that Kafka was the mole, I wanted to read
more Kafka.

I played Irmgard [Keun] for my role play, and I think now that she is
important to me. This is the reason why I made an exit to her [room].
Perhaps, because she is not as well-known as Kafka, Mann or Luxemburg, it is
good to make an exit to Irmgard. Although she does not have as strong
opinions as Rosa Luxemburg, she is also fascinating.

I built an exit to Stefan's room. I interpreted it and gave him a present. His
autobiography contains many insights into life, which caused me to reflect on
my childhood. Stefan's life is similar to the lives of the authors [that we read].
Stefan and the authors lived in countries with political unrest. Thomas Mass,
Irmgard Keun, and Rosa Luxemburg experienced the Nazis, while Stefan
experienced a communist government.

Although written by a student with some of the weakest linguistic skills in the
class, this essay is nonetheless impressive for what it conveys about the variety, depth, and richness of her reading practices at the low-intermediate level.
Like nearly every other student in the class, Lucy chose a combination of
student writing (Nora's room and Stefan's self-description) and course readings (Kafka, Keun, and Lasker-Schüler). She also cites Thomas Mann and
Rosa Luxemburg. More significant, however, is the range of reading practices

she cites to explain these choices. Her exit to Lasker-Schüler's room emphasizes her pleasure in the multiplicity of meanings that result from the collaborative reading process, while her "tunnel" to Kafka's room stresses a similar
pleasure in the play of uncovering textual secrets hidden in the text. (Tunnel
is a metaphor we introduced in the assignment. Of course, it is particularly
appropriate in terms of Kafka's text, which is about a mole's paranoid relation to his burrow.)

Lucy's connections to texts are also highly personal and complex. Playing
Keun in the role play, for instance, gave her a personal connection to that
author that seems not to have originated in the first reading of that text—so
personal, in fact, that Keun is the only published author she cites by first
name. In fact, Lucy's connection to the text might say more about her own
quiet and shy demeanor in class, particularly when we worked outside the
MOO, since her explanation rests less on an identification with Keun's active
and distinctively modern heroine or even Keun's own rich and politically
irreverent biography than on her (correct) perception that Keun has been
overlooked and underappreciated in comparison to her peers. Calinescu suggests that such personal identifications with authors and texts reflect "the circularity of the reader's time as opposed to our habitual historical consciousness of an inflexibly linear, unidirectional time" (1993, p. 53). For instance,
although Lucy shares with her classmates an enthusiasm for Radiohead, her
decision to link her room with Nora's stems from a new appreciation of
Radiohead's social criticism as an extension of the battle of early twentieth-
century German artists and intellectuals against the restrictive bourgeois
conventions of the time, one of the themes that Lucy repeatedly identified in
the various course readings. Likewise, she selects Stefan's self-description not
only for its intertextuality with the German texts of authors who confronted
National Socialism but also for the way that it causes her to return to her own
childhood.

Concluding Remarks

Although even students with relatively weak language skills proved
adept at describing complex reading practices in the target language, we also
required students to reflect in English on their writing, reading, and learning
as part of our effort to achieve sustained self-reflection over the course of the
semester. These English-language reflections accompanied their learning
portfolio, which consisted of printouts of all their writings in the MOO (in
their various versions) as well as other assignments completed outside the
MOO, such as grammar exercises and personal vocabulary lists. Intended as a

general statement about their overall language learning during the semester, the final self-reflection assignment nevertheless produced many outstanding testimonies on the impact of these reading practices, including this excerpt from Annette:

> My work with the language this semester has heightened my love for it and my desire to come to a deeper understanding of it. This is due to the way in which the class entirely changed my view of language acquisition. Through the texts we read, as well as the study of the Weimar Republic, the articles and the ideas of our own classmates, I have come to understand that language is much more than a spoken word. It is also about culture and literature, and about exploring and finding our own selves within a new medium. This understanding has made German so much more exciting for me, and it makes me so much more eager to continue in my study of the language. . . . Equally important are the ways in which my study of German this semester has actually helped me in all aspects of my life. Our concentration on identity has forced me to look within myself more than I normally would have, and it has helped me to understand myself and to use this understanding to aid in different areas of my life. Through study of different texts, I've learned that, though I'm a non-native speaker, I can still bring about my own inferences and opinions towards German literature. Knowing this makes the study of texts so much more exciting for me, and I now feel so much more confident and capable in my reading and analysis. This also extends to literature in my own native language. I find myself more readily reading into the many different meanings that a piece of literature presents, and I am much more open to the many different possibilities that can be found within it.

In addition to our readings in German, students also read over the course of the semester a number of articles in second language acquisition research, including Kramsch's "Privilege" essay. Our goal in assigning these texts was to give students the ideas and vocabulary to reflect critically and independently on their language learning and to involve them as collaborators with us in helping to set the direction of the course. Although the activities of this course inspired Annette in part to spend her junior year studying in Vienna, her sense of the reading and language study that took place in the course is not limited to its practical benefits for engaging with members of the target culture. Instead, she points to a richer, perhaps liberating, sense of pleasure, knowledge, and self that emerges from the collaborative, experiential, and circular reading practices. Annette identifies the ideas of her fellow students alongside the texts themselves as a source for her new understanding of language study, which she explicitly defines as more than oral proficiency and which she implicitly portrays as involving more than communication. In her description, reading exceeds classification as a mere skill among others. Instead, the act of reading becomes a profound set of experiences with texts—experiences that lead beyond particular knowledge about a specific text or about German texts to emerge as a way of experiencing, well, experience itself—in the form of reflections on identity, the self, and the very engagement with culture, regardless of language. In the end, Annette's notions of reading emerge from language learning and continue to inform her understanding of language acquisition. They also incorporate into a third-semester course the rich notions of reading that are the hallmark of literary studies, cultural studies, and other upper-level courses.

We do not wish to claim that this kind of productive, imaginative foreign language reading at the intermediate level can only occur in the MOO, since most literary critics suggest that there is no other way to read complex texts. The point is not to make technologies such as the MOO the privileged site of a new pedagogy. Rather, if, as Richard Kern predicts, "the most profound effects of computer technology on literacy and language learning will likely arise . . . from the new forms of information dissemination and social interaction made possible by local and global computing networks" (Kern 2000, p. 237), then it becomes valuable and necessary to explore, identify, and harness the productive benefits of network-based language technologies. In our case, using the MOO enabled us to rethink the possibilities for low-intermediate reading in much the same way as our students: as a collaboration between ourselves and our students, as a set of experiences that required constant reflection throughout the semester, and as a process of returning again and again to our students' writings, discussions, and reflections as well as the primary texts. Together our students have produced a series of readings and texts that remain in the MOO as invitations to subsequent users to, in Joyce's words, "join with us in shapeful behavior" and recognize "how meaning is made" (2000, p. 43). In our MOO, students' rooms and writings remain unless or until the student decides to recycle or delete his or her objects. There are now several generations of student rooms in MOOssiggang.

More important than the MOO itself are the theoretical and practical insights that can be derived from its use as a means of foregrounding for students the essentially collaborative, experiential, and circular nature of reading. It is interesting that in her statement, Annette only refers obliquely and indirectly to the MOO ("a new medium") and focuses instead on the benefits derived from that experience "in all aspects of my life," even the experience of reading in her native language. In this manner, Annette not only lays claim to the fundamental importance of foreign language study for a broad liberal arts education but she reverses the traditional trajectory of reading development as proceeding unidirectionally from one's native language to the foreign language, suggesting instead that students might actually become better readers in their first language by learning to read critically and creatively in the second. Likewise, we want to emphasize that the MOO helped establish a paradigm for reading in the intermediate foreign language classroom based on approaches to reading that are typically reserved for upper-level classes in the foreign language or for classes conducted in English. This semester-long approach to foreign language reading promises to make even lower-level courses part of the broader liberal arts curriculum, since it seeks to impart life-long critical thinking skills as well as practical language skills. But it also expanded for us our own sense of what students are capable of achieving at the low-intermediate level, especially since students' ability to articulate thoughtful intertextual connections and reflect on the reading process not only occurred in the students' English-language statements but also in the German-language texts they produced in response to the course readings. Ultimately, we believe that the collaborative experience of literally and figuratively entering the web of texts produced in our class gave our students a profound new sense of what reading in the foreign language can really mean and do.

Acknowledgments

We thank Peter Patrikis, Michael Joyce, Amanda Thornton, and our co-teacher at Williams College, Valerie Weinstein, for their enthusiastic support of our work and the students of Vassar College's German 210 and Williams College's German 103 for their patience and willingness to experiment. We also acknowledge the Steering Committee of the Vassar-Williams Mellon Grant on Teaching with Technology in the Foreign Languages for funding this collaborative venture.

Notes

1. See Selfe and Hilligoss (1994) for an overview of parallel efforts in one of the other traditionally skills-based areas of the liberal arts curriculum, English composition, that have productively used computers to integrate some of the diverse theoretical insights from literary and cultural studies into their teaching, research agenda, and endeavors to reform the curriculum.

2. Our German-language MOO is called MOOssiggang and can be accessed via Netscape™ 4.5 (or higher) or Microsoft Explorer™ 5.0 (or higher) with the URL ⟨http://iberia.vassar.edu:7000⟩. Our MOO core, which represents the latest generation of MOOs, is open source freeware developed by Jan Rune Holmevik and Cynthia Haynes, the

creators of LinguaMOO, which is based at the University of Texas at Dallas. The en-Core MOO Educational Core Database can be downloaded free of charge from the LinguaMOO website ⟨http://lingua.utdallas.edu⟩. For an overview of other educational uses of the MOO, see Haynes and Holmevik 1998. Their student guide, *MOOniversity,* is also an excellent resource for beginners.

3. In an earlier version of this class, in which a few of the same texts were used, students explicitly asked for more background on the primary texts. Based on this feedback, we decided to make available excerpts from secondary materials about the authors, their texts, and the time period. After an initial reading of the primary German-language texts, students returned to discuss them a second time in small groups after they had a chance to draw on the secondary sources to help expand their readings of the primary texts. In this case, one of the background texts dealt with Mann's homosexuality.

References

Beauvois, M. H. (1992). Computer-Assisted Classroom Discussion in the Foreign Language Classroom: Conversation in Slow Motion. *Foreign Language Annals* 25: 455–63.

——. (1994). E-Talk: Attitudes and Motivation in Computer-Assisted Classroom Discussion. *Computers and the Humanities* 28: 177–90.

——. (1997). Computer-Mediated Communication: Technology for Improving Speaking and Writing. In *Technology-Enhanced Language Learning,* edited by M. D. Bush, pp. 165–82. Lincolnwood, Ill.: National Textbook.

Berman, R. (1994). Global Thinking, Local Teaching: Departments, Curricula and Culture. *ADFL Bulletin* 26(1): 7–11.

Calinescu, M. (1993). *Rereading.* New Haven: Yale University Press.

Doughty, C., and J. Williams, eds. (1998). *Focus on Form in Classroom Second Language Acquisition.* Cambridge: Cambridge University Press.

Eagleton, T. (1983). *Literary Theory: An Introduction.* Minneapolis: University of Minnesota Press.

Haynes, C., and J. R. Holmevik, eds. (1998). *High Wired: On the Design, Use, and Theory of Educational MOOs.* Ann Arbor: University of Michigan Press.

Holmevik, J. R., and C. Haynes, eds. (2000). *LinguaMoo.* University of Texas, Dallas, 20 March 2000 ⟨http://lingua.utdallas.edu⟩.

——. (2000). *MOOniversity.* Boston: Allyn and Bacon.

Joyce, M. (2000). MOO or Mistakenness. In *Othermindedness: The Emergence of Network Culture,* pp. 35–48. Ann Arbor: University of Michigan Press.

Kafka, F. (1946). Der Bau. In *Gesammelte Schriften,* edited by Max Brod. 5: 172–214. New York: Schocken.

Kern, R. (1995). Redefining the Boundaries of Foreign Language Literacy. In *Redefining the Boundaries of Language Study,* edited by C. Kramsch, pp. 61–98. Boston: Heinle & Heinle.

——. (1998). Technology, Social Interaction, and FL Literacy. In *New Ways of Learning and Teaching: Focus on Technology and Foreign Language Education,* edited by J. A. Muyskens, pp. 57–92. Boston: Heinle & Heinle.

———. (2000). *Literacy and Language Teaching.* Oxford: Oxford University Press.

Keun, I. (1979). *Das kunstseidene Mädchen.* Bergisch Gladbach: Gustav Lübbe Verlag.

Kohonen, V. (1992). Experiential Language Learning: Second Language Learning as Cooperative Learner Education. In *Collaborative Language Learning and Teaching,* edited by D. Nunan, pp. 14–39. Cambridge: Cambridge University Press.

Kramsch, C. (1997). The Privilege of the Nonnative Speaker. *PMLA* 112: 359–69.

Kramsch, C., F. A'Ness, and W. S. E. Lam. (2000). Authenticity and Authorship in the Computer-Mediated Acquisition of L2 Literacy. *Language Learning & Technology* 4(20): 75–104.

Kramsch, C., and T. Nolden. (1994). Redefining Literacy in a Foreign Language. *Die Unterrichtspraxis/Teaching German* 27(1): 28–35.

Lasker-Schüler, E. (1984). Weltflucht. In *Gesammelte Gedichte,* edited by F. Kemp, p. 49. Darmstadt: Wissenschaftliche Buchgesellschaft.

Lee, J. F., and A. Valdman, eds. (2000). *Form and Meaning: Multiple Perspectives.* Boston: Heinle & Heinle.

Mann, T. (1976). Im Spiegel. In *Deutsches Lesebuch: Von Luther bis Liebknecht,* edited by S. Hermling, pp. 533–37. Leipzig: Verlag Philipp Reclam.

Roche, J. M., and M. J. Webber. (1995). *Für- und Wider-Sprüche: Eine Integriertes Text-Buch für Colleges und Universitäten.* New Haven: Yale University Press.

Rott, S. (2000). Relationships Between the Process of Reading, Word Inferencing, and Incidental Word Acquisition. In *Form and Meaning: Multiple Perspectives,* edited by J. F. Lee and A. Valdman, pp. 255–82. Boston: Heinle & Heinle.

Schneider, J., and S. von der Emde. (2000). Brave New (Virtual) World: Transforming Language Learning into Cultural Studies through Online Learning Environments (MOOs). *ADFL Bulletin* 32(1): 18–26.

Sedgwick, E. K. (1990). *Epistemology of the Closet.* Berkeley: University of California Press.

Selfe, C. L., and S. Hilligoss, eds. (1994). *Literacy and Computers: The Complications of Teaching and Learning with Technology.* New York: Modern Language Association.

Swaffar, J. K., K. M. Arens, and H. Byrnes. (1991). *Reading for Meaning: An Integrated Approach to Language Learning.* Englewood Cliffs, N.J.: Prentice-Hall.

Turkle, S. (1995). *Life on the Screen: Identity in the Age of the Internet.* New York: Simon & Schuster.

von der Emde, S., and J. Schneider, eds. (2000). *MOOssiggang.* Vassar College, 21 March 2000 ⟨http://iberia.vassar.edu:7000⟩.

von der Emde, S., J. Schneider, and M. Kötter. (2001). Technically Speaking: Transforming Language Learning Through Virtual Learning Environments (MOOs). *Modern Language Journal* 85(2): 210–25.

Warschauer, M., and R. Kern, eds. (2000). *Network-Based Language Teaching: Concepts and Practice.* Cambridge: Cambridge University Press.

8

Double-Booked: Translation, Simultaneity, and Duplicity in the Foreign Literature Classroom

MARK WEBBER

Introduction

The German word *Orchideenfächer* refers to academic subjects that are as beautiful and endangered as rare orchids—and as removed as these flowers from the political and practical concerns of daily life. Although English lacks a one-word equivalent, teachers of foreign language and literature in North America can instantly sense the metaphor's double import. It suggests that what we do, lovely though it may be, does not connect with or influence the real world in the same way that engineering, for example, does. According to this metaphor, there is a unidirectional barrier between our disciplines and the real world. That barrier prevents us from influencing the real world, but it does not shield us from that world's depredations. What is worse, our purported separation from that world counts as a liability when real-world concerns (such as student-teacher ratios and in-field employment rates of graduates) provide the criteria for academic decisions.

The lack of reciprocity inherent in the metaphor's dual thrust leads teachers of foreign language to practice. Indeed, we must come to terms with multiple duplicities that involve and question the theoretical, ethical, and pedagogical bases of the profession even as they engage the duplicitous politics of the academy and of society at large.

In this chapter I examine those duplicities as both challenges and opportunities for the teaching of foreign language literacy. I do so by presenting a case study of twinned courses—one in English and one in the target language—on the writings of Franz Kafka. After explaining my terminology, particularly with reference to the paper's title, I shall sketch the political and institutional framework within which the courses originated. I then focus on the students, subject matter, and underlying pedagogical approach of these courses. In the final section I consider the roles of translation and metaphor with the broader theoretical and pedagogical context of foreign language teaching and learning. Throughout, the chapter raises questions of not only *whom* we are teaching, but *what* we are teaching them and *why*.

Terminology

What does the title mean by "double-booked"? First, as teachers, scholars, and administrators, we are increasingly under pressure to do multitasking. Sometimes, when there are not enough hours in the day or students in the classrooms, we are required to be in two places at one time. That is one of the things to which the title adverts, and it is one of the pressures to which the Kafka courses respond. Second, being "double-booked" refers to the fact that in order to teach twinned courses, one must ensure that the reading list is available in both German and English and that the marks go to the right office for the right students. In this context keeping two sets of books is an administrative necessity. Here as in the field of accounting, however, keeping two sets of books may strike us as a dubious practice that requires investigation, whether forensic or academic. Third and most important, the phrase "double booked" should be understood metaphorically, also in a double sense: as a figurative expression for being in two mental spaces at the same time and as a metaphor for the way in which metaphor itself functions.

These notions of doubleness tie in directly to the key words of the subtitle: *translation, simultaneity, and duplicity.* Of course, the idea of mentioning the first two words in relation to each other arose as a typically bad pun on simultaneous translation. Yet even this pun provides an opportunity to question both the phrase and its constituent elements. First, there is translation itself, which, if translated into Greek, comes out looking quite like the word metaphor (μεταφορα): both denote a kind of carrying over from one realm to another; or, to put it metaphorically and somewhat differently, both require being in two places at one time (see Godard 1990, p. 22). Second, there is the notion of simultaneity. Anyone who has experienced simultaneous translation—or more accurately, simultaneous interpretation—knows that it is anything but simultaneous. Does the claim of simultaneity, then, like the notion of double-booking, also involve the third term of the subtitle, duplicity? Again, this is itself a duplicitous term, for *duplicity* means, first, and in common parlance, dishonesty. A duplicitous statement is not what it purports to be. In this sense, there is *less* to it than meets the eye. Simultaneously, however, it signals gemination, a doubling that resists being brought together. The double valence of *duplicity* raises the following questions: To what extent do the Kafka courses, and courses like them, provide *value added* by doing more than one thing at one time? To what extent are they frauds perpetrated on students, academic administrators, and ourselves?

Finally, there is the potential duplicity of this paper itself, plowing as it does a double path that steers simultaneously for the Scylla of "show-and-tell" and the Charybdis of abstraction in the name of theory, and all with the hope of avoiding both. Since, however, I cannot *describe* both headings simultaneously, I shall begin by tacking toward Scylla.

The Frame

The framework for university language teaching in North America is changing, and nowhere is it changing more dramatically and (potentially) more dangerously than in the Province of Ontario. In my own field of German, several departments or programs have already been shut down; others are "on probation," either from their own institutions or from provincially mandated oversight bodies; and still others know that where the action of university administrations will not close them, inaction and attrition will. The problem is not limited to German or to Ontario. In response to expressions of concern from around the country, the Humanities and Social Sciences Federation of Canada (HSSFC) has convened a special working group both to analyze where we are and to recommend where we should be going.

Ordinarily I would not dignify the attitude of the government of the Province of Ontario toward what we do for a living by acknowledging it. But because, like Everest (or Scylla, perhaps), it is there, and because it is both symptomatic and profoundly constitutive of the conditions in which we work, I will mention it. Briefly, the premier (the equivalent of the governor) of Ontario has made it abundantly clear that, from his perspective, the humanities and social sciences are irrelevant, and the only thing that matters is computer science along with allied disciplines. The Ontario Ministry of Training, Colleges, and Universities—the sequence here is significant, especially since, in Canadian parlance, a college is not (yet) a degree-granting institution of higher learning but a polytechnic—is increasingly directing how the publicly financed universities of the province use provincial funding. Universities that resist run the risk of being punished financially.

No matter how sympathetic a dean is (and ours is genuinely sympathetic), there is increased and increasing pressure to ensure that the courses we offer actually attract students. In responding to the Dean's Office, departments and individual faculty members may not see eye to eye. Those of us who teach in departments of foreign languages and literatures work with the consequences of changes in the secondary schools. (French, as one of Canada's official languages and a mandated subject, is not a foreign language in this context.) If a declining number of students enroll in a foreign language in high school, that means that of the declining number of students who enroll in a language at university, still fewer come to us with the background to work in nontranslated literature, at least at the beginning. Moreover, as someone who also teaches a first-year foundations course that looks at animals in the literary imagination—a course in the Division of Humanities that explicitly teaches critical thinking, organizational, and writing skills—I can confirm the obvious: the overall literacy skills of our students, however we may wish to characterize them, present the context in which we work also in the foreign languages.

The Focus

What does all this mean for the specific courses that serve as my case study? At first glance, the humanities course, taught in English, might seem to be an unremarkable example of the species of course that has existed for decades, the kind we call literature in translation. For as long as enrollment has been the battleground, literature in translation has been the answer to English departments or Divisions of Humanities that have been, to use a loaded word, poaching our game. There is an interesting displacement at work here, however. The English departments do not usually consider these courses to be, let us say, *German* literature in translation. They consider them simply as literature courses, part of their academic franchise. It is we who use the phrase *in translation* as both a come-on to prospective students— "No knowledge of German required"—and as a concessive, almost self-flagellatory, signal to ourselves: "I know it's not the real thing, but I have no choice."

In fact, the Kafka courses have a slightly different history. The Division of Humanities at York is an interdisciplinary teaching unit in the Faculty of Arts. Humanities courses are key elements of our general education requirements, and the division is the home of several interdisciplinary programs such as religious studies and German studies. (The Kafka course counts toward the major requirements of both programs.) The division also has an undergraduate major in its own right, to which may soon be added a graduate program. Having been cross-appointed between German and Humanities since the late 1970s, in the early 1980s I introduced a full-year course on Kafka for Humanities within the rubric "Writers in Their Age." The course satisfied both upper-level general education requirements, as they were then constituted, and major requirements for both Humanities and Religious Studies. A few years later, I developed, within the curriculum of the Department of Languages, Literatures, and Linguistics, a half-course in German that also centered on Kafka. The two courses had different numbers, different clienteles, and different foci, and they were offered in different years. Only in the 1990s, when the pressures to which I have alluded became more severe, did they come together in their present duplicity.

That constellation brings me back to the questions I enumerated at the beginning of this essay: Whom are we teaching? What are we teaching them? and why? By asking whom, I am not simply reverting to the question of the preparation of students entering university in the twenty-first century. Sitting in my classroom, or potentially attracted to it, are several groupings of students whose backgrounds, interests, and needs differ in crucial respects. In order of numbers, the humanities students predominate. Because the shape of the Faculty of Arts curriculum has changed since the inception of the humanities course, students no longer enroll in order to fulfill their upper-level general education requirements. The Humanities, German Studies, and Religious Studies majors taking the course for major credit—and English, creative writing, philosophy, and fine arts students who enroll in it as an elective—constitute the great majority of course members. They are in the course because they want to be, and they are among the brightest and most interesting students in the Faculty. Only in rare cases do they know German. The students who enroll through German may or may not be native speakers, and sad to say, they are not all that often the best and the brightest. In the context of my training, the conference for which this essay came into being, and the Consortium that organized it, it seems obvious that I should be concentrating on the students who enroll in the German course. In fact, I will be arguing that to give priority to the students enrolled through German is a mistake, even from the perspective of foreign language teaching.

My answer to the question "Whom are we teaching?" is intertwined with the next question: What are we teaching them? Since the end of World War II (or before), the question of what we are teaching our students has received changing answers. Probably not many of my readers were on the receiving end of the so-called grammar-translation approach, although translation exercises and tests are still important parts of the high-school and university foreign language curricula in Germany. In North America, I would venture the guess that the word *translation* occurs in course descriptions primarily in two contexts: first, in courses or curricula dedicated to developing skills in translating as an expertise and profession in its own right, and second, in the context of literature in translation.

As we know, however, there is a constant rebalancing of priorities within the profession of foreign language teaching, and over the past several years there has been a rekindling of interest in reading as a skill and a pedagogy; the conference for which this essay was conceived simultaneously reflected that interest and sought to influence the debate. From my perspective much progress has been made in recognizing that (1) reading involves and invokes processes and skills that are also entailed in producing and responding to spoken language; (2) reading in a second or foreign language is a particular case of intercultural understanding that entails the same techniques and processes as those used in responding to other intercultural phenomena; and (3) reading and intercultural understanding are analogous processes that are not "passive" or "receptive" but active and creative (Webber 1993, p. 3).

Seen in this way, foreign language literacy is a special case of literacy in general, but it also highlights aspects of literacy that may get lost in courses dealing with first-language textuality. All of this takes place in the context of a liberal arts agenda that is increasingly under attack. Clifford Adelman's description of a developmental model of foreign language education that situates it within a larger approach to university teaching is still relevant (Adelman 1984, p. 115):

> The developmental model respects the notional-functional approach to learning and the needs of students—from gathering information to suasion—in real cultural contexts. The drive of the developmental model is toward student autonomy, toward tolerance for ambiguity and complexity, and toward the perception of an instructor as a resource (not as an external, authoritative repository of knowledge). In Arthur Chickering's words, the model drives toward the capacity to generate paradigms, insights, judgments, and to reorganize past conceptions on the basis of new experiences. The role of curriculum under that model, Chickering would say, is to pose key dilemmas to students.

Conceptually, pedagogically, and politically, to exempt ourselves and our students from this curricular responsibility is to sell ourselves and them short. We become complicitous in reducing language teaching to a non-academic, technical activity, thus reinforcing the marginality of language programs within the university. This reduction takes place when our programs face a contradictory situation. They are simultaneously under mounting pressure to demonstrate that they deserve a valued place as contributors to the core intellectual mission of the university, and they have the means to do so. This contradiction is matched by another. For at the same time as language pedagogy is becoming more content-based and—dare we say it?—more academic, the university, at least in Ontario, is in the process of becoming less academic and more technical. Are our trajectories converging? Will they shoot past each other, merge, or collide, bringing each other down?

Similar questions about convergence, merging, or mutual destruction presented themselves with reference to the two original courses on Kafka, one taught exclusively in German and one taught exclusively in English, in the sense that these were the languages of the texts as well as of the classroom. In the end, I opted for duplicity. There would be twin courses, each with its own number and reading list, and each taught in its own language.

Logistically, the trick (and I use the word consciously) was to find a way of teaching the courses simultaneously, not just during the same academic term but literally at the same time. Only in this way would there be enough students, through combining the enrollments, to justify the offering. Only in this way could the German section provide sufficient courses at the upper level to allow our majors to take honors degrees. So I came to be double-booked: with two courses, two class lists, two grade books, two reading lists, and one classroom. Actually, this is not quite true: because the group meets together for three hours per week, and because most of the students do not know German, the plenary meetings are held in English. Still, the students enrolled through German do their readings and most of their written work in German. In any case, I meet with them for an extra hour per week to take up, in German, issues specific to the German texts.

The words "the students enrolled through German do their readings . . . in German" arose almost automatically from the keyboard. Saying this was duplicitous, though not consciously so. To be more accurate: The students are assigned the texts in German, but do they really read the German texts? And do I really expect them to? The answer has two levels: one descriptive, the other prescriptive. Some of these students do read only the German texts, because to read the English texts, too, would take more time. It is clear, however, that many of them read the English texts as their primary source, while skimming the German texts because they know we will be discussing them in the class time reserved for this purpose.

A Gaggle of Geese, a Duplicity of Texts

This section of the chapter picks up on discrepancy between description and prescription, which also reveals a gap between theory and practice. To do so requires reading Kafka as a special case of literacy, and this special case involves a brief detour into Kafka-land.

One of the most difficult issues in dealing with Kafka is the state of the text. Until the critical edition began appearing in the 1980s, many of the texts we had—the texts that had made Kafka into the best-selling author he became decades after his death—were not authentic. That is one reason why my course syllabi claim that Kafka is one of the most widely read and most widely misunderstood authors in the canon of university courses in literature, philosophy, religious studies, and political science.

Kafka became known in North America on the basis of his novels, particularly through the novel usually called in English *The Trial*, but also through *The Castle*. The problem is that he completed neither of these manuscripts. His literary executor, Max Brod, ignored Kafka's instructions to destroy all unpublished works and edited and published them both, along with other unfinished texts, in such a way as to protect and enhance the image of his friend—at least as Brod imagined that image. The received Kafka canon, therefore, is based on duplicity, in the second sense of the word and perhaps also in the first. The first act of translation that we as readers and teachers have to undertake with respect to such works, then, is to translate back from the canonical text to the authorial text, or as close as we can get to it. As affordable editions with more reliable texts become available, it is possible to dispense with tables that show how the structure of a work has been rearranged by Brod from that in the manuscript. Part of reading is thinking about the status of the text, however, and so this is a practice that also has a pedagogical justification, whatever edition we are reading.

The pedagogy involves demonstrating—and having the students respond to—the notion that reading is not a passive process but involves active creativity on the part of the reader. One way of approaching this notion is to show that the text itself is not a product but a process, something that leads us also from the level of organization to that of word meaning, since the word by which Kafka referred to his novel, *Der Process*, means both "trial" and "process." Another way of illustrating this notion to the students is to confront them with various of Kafka's false starts (or trial runs) or major variants from his manuscripts (for example, Kafka 1992, p. 343). These texts interact with one another in a way that makes it obvious that any notions of the linear order of reading are misplaced; they make it necessary and possible for the students to make sense by creating their own order among and for the texts.

A major problem with translations of Kafka is that his language is metaphorical in a special way. He often uses what I call radical metaphor, which activates the slumbering etymological root of the expression and thereby revivifies what might be overlooked as figuration or might otherwise be taken as dead metaphor (see Harman 1996, p. 300 and p. 310, n. 30). A famous example is the word *ungeheuer,* commonly translated as "monstrous" or "gigantic" when it appears in a Kafka text published during his lifetime. In the story known as *The Metamorphosis,* the protagonist, Gregor Samsa, awakes to find himself transformed into a huge beetle. *Ungeheuer* here is an adjective describing that bug. (I shall not recount the secondary literature on the subject. See the summary in Corngold 1973, p. 11 and the etymology and definitions in Grimm 1984.) The root of the word has to do with *home-iness,* so that its negation, which Kafka utilizes, comes to mean huge and monstrous (that is, abnormal in size, shape, and appearance) by virtue of not being part of the family, not being housebroken, so to speak. Gregor as bug is, so far as his family and employer are concerned, outside the bounds of the familiar, beyond the pale. Without coming close to a full reading of the story, I would assert that Gregor's transformation into a spineless creature (as he calls his superior at work) is an expression of both his punishment for and his redemption from his life. Gregor is not at home with himself or his family, but neither he nor they are aware of this condition until his so-called metamorphosis. But this is not an occasion to interpret Kafka, so let us return to issues of language.

In the conference presentation of this essay, I asked participants what they had thought of when they heard the phrase "beyond the pale." Like them, I had thought of the Pale of Settlement, an overtly discriminatory corpus of legislation that restricted the places of residence of Jews to the Russian provinces, which had been annexed from Poland, and to New Russia (Klier 1986, p. 75). The *OED,* however, lists the noun *pale* in no less than seven senses, deriving from the original meaning of *stake,* "a pointed piece of wood intended to be driven into the ground, esp. as used with others to form a fence" (*OED,* 1971, 2:390). By extension, the word comes to designate the enclosure, literal or figurative, demarcated by that fence. To be *beyond* the pale, then, is to be out of those bounds. What does this have to do with reading in a foreign language? It illustrates some of the methods that we and our students should be practicing in support of both the general and specific goals of literacy toward which our courses, in the target language, in translation, and in the interstices between them, should be striving.

For the students of both German and humanities, it is effective, in this context, to let them work with texts as (1) *intertexts,* texts by Kafka and others that challenge students and allow them to make connections, and (2) as *interlanguage* between German and English. A short example will be instructive here. The etymology of *ungeheuer* is significant, but it can also be the subject of a lecture in either German or English. What is more interesting and pedagogically productive is to juxtapose texts, as in examples (1) and (2).

(1) I ordered my horse brought from the stable. The servant did not understand me. I went into the stable myself, saddled my horse and mounted it. In the distance I heard a trumpet sounding; I asked him what it meant. He knew nothing and had heard nothing. At the gate he detained me and asked: Where are you riding to, Master? I don't know, I said; just away from here, just away from here. Incessantly away from here, only in this way can I reach my goal. So you know your goal? he asked. Yes, I answered, I already said: Away-from-Here, that is my goal. You don't have any provisions along, he said. I don't need any, I said; The journey is so long that I must starve to death if, on the way, I don't get anything. No provision can save me. For happily, you know, it is a truly *monstrous* journey.
(Kafka 1983, p. 449)

Ich befahl mein Pferd aus dem Stall zu holen. Der Diener verstand mich nicht. Ich ging selbst in den Stall, sattelte mein Pferd und bestieg es. In der Ferne hörte ich eine Trompete blasen, ich fragte ihn, was das bedeute. Er wußte nichts und hatte nichts gehört. Beim Tore hielt er mich auf und fragte: +Wohin reitest Du, Herr? *Ich weiß es nicht*, sagte ich, +nur weg von hier, nur weg von hier. Immerfort weg von hier, nur so kann ich mein Ziel erreichen.* +Du kennst also Dein Ziel?* fragte er. +Ja*, antwortete ich, +ich sagte es doch, Weg-von-hier, das ist mein Ziel. +Du hast keinen Eßvorrat mit*, sagte er. +Ich brauche keinen*, sagte ich, +die Reise ist so lang, daß ich verhungern muß, wenn ich auf dem Weg nichts bekomme. Kein Eßvorrat kann mich retten. Es ist ja zum Glück eine wahrhaft *ungeheuere* Reise.* (Kafka 1986, p. 384)

(2) *The Next Village*
My grandfather used to say: Life is astonishingly short. Now in my memory it compresses itself such that I can scarcely comprehend, for example, how a young person can resolve to ride into the next village without fearing that even discounting **unhappy** coincidences

Das nächste Dorf
Mein Großvater pflegte zu sagen: +Das Leben ist erstaunlich kurz. Jetzt in der Erinnerung drängt es sich mir so zusammen, daß ich zum Beispiel kaum begreife, wie ein junger Mensch sich entschließen kann ins nächste Dorf zu reiten, ohne zu fürchten, daß von **un-**

even the time of a normal, **happily** passing life will not suffice by far for such a ride. (Kafka 1983, p. 404)	glücklichen Zufällen ganz abgesehen schon die Zeit des gewöhnlichen, **glücklich** ablaufenden Lebens für einen solchen Ritt bei weitem nicht hinreicht.* (Kafka 1996, p. 342)

Working in small groups, the class can make connections of intertext and interlanguage, connections that in turn raise questions (I have boldfaced, italicized, and otherwise marked certain connections in the texts to illustrate some of the possibilities). For the students who do not know German, the course provides a bridge, and perhaps some incentive, to learning it. For the students who do know German, questions not only about Kafka's German lexicon but also of the adequacy of the translation point to interpretative issues.

Instead of attempting to make the text transparent, this approach thickens the text by doubling it. This doubling is not simply a question of pointing out to students when a translation is, in my opinion, "wrong," or when it does not pick up on strands in Kafka's language. Interestingly, the sessions held in German often begin with questions from the students about single words, and the language of the sessions, though predominantly German, sometimes switches to English and sometimes reverts to the interlanguage we call *Genglish*.

The doubling of language as an attempt to be in two places at one time, *to double-book,* as my title would have it, includes a resistance to being *im-paled,* fenced in, restricted to a single position. As shown in example 3, Kafka speaks to this in his metaphor of *Einpfählen,* which insists on its own metaphoricity through the duplicitous use of the word apparent *(scheinbar).*

(3) All human errors are impatience, the premature breaking off of what is methodical, an apparent **fencing in** of the apparent thing. (Kafka 1991, p. 15)	Alle menschlichen Fehler sind Ungeduld, ein unzeitiges Abbrechen des Methodischen, ein scheinbares **Einpfählen** der scheinbaren Sache. (Kafka 1992, p. 32)

The fencing in, or impaling, of which Kafka speaks is apparent, precisely because both the circumscription and the item being circumscribed lack essence. On one hand, then, the error is categorical, a mistaking of the husk for the kernel. On the other, it is not beyond redemption since the error itself must be superficial only. Any limitation that one can impose applies to that which is already limited; the infinite cannot be boxed in.

The degree to which Kafka lends himself to the pedagogical approach I am describing and advocating becomes even clearer in another set of Kafka texts that revolve around issues of stability, unity, and duplicity. The following examples illustrate Kafka's own duplicity in geminating texts that resist final form. At the same time, he reiterates the notion that truth is indivisible. The good news is that it exists and that it can be perceived to exist; the bad news is that in order to accomplish this perception, one must be outside the pale, the pale that truth cannot in any case abide.

(4) There are only two things. Truth and lies. Truth is indivisible, hence it cannot recognize itself; anyone who wants to recognize it has to be a lie. (Kafka 1991, p. 35)	Es gibt nur zweierlei: Wahrheit und Lüge. Die Wahrheit ist unteilbar, kann sich also selbst nicht erkennen. Wer sie erkennen will muß Lüge sein. (Kafka 1992, p. 69)
(5) Truth is indivisible, and thus cannot itself know itself; he who wants to know her must be Du-plicity. (Kafka 1991, p. 35)	Wahrheit ist unteilbar, kann sich also selbst nicht erkennen; wer sie erkennen will, muß Lüge sein. (Kafka, 1992, p. 130)

As these examples suggest, the thematic and conceptual ties between Kafka as thinker and writer and a double-booking, double-dealing, bifurcated, forked-tongued course about him are multiple. Despite Max Brod's attempts to create Kafka the novelist, Kafka was most prolific as a writer of short texts, many of them fragmentary beginnings in his notebooks that beg for completion. They lend themselves in length and open structure to creative responses from students whose first language is not German. They place issues of language and textuality in the foreground, both implicitly and explicitly. The history of their editing and translation is itself on the table for discussion. And a major theme for Kafka is precisely duplicity, again itself in twofold sense. First, as seen in examples 1, 2, 4, and 5, there is the effort to be in two places at one time, places we can term life and death, or the spiritual and the physical, or the eternal and temporal realms, pursuit and patience, essence and appearance. There is a tendency to use terms that are themselves metaphors, though metaphors that resist the human impatience to arrive at certainty by conflating the metaphorical tenor and vehicle, in part by virtue of their apparent lack of the tenor (see Webber 1995, p. 7). Second, there is the consciousness of duplicity, of the opposition between unity and duality, which is both a structural and thematic element of Kafka's thought and writing.

Metaphor and Translation: Singularity and Unidirectionality

Earlier, I remarked on the affinity of the two terms and concepts of *metaphor* and *translation*. Both are duplicitous in that they require us to be in two linguistic and conceptual realms at the same time. From my perspective, both are quintessentially interpretive and persuasive (rhetorical) operations that lie at the heart of language and cognition. Making their workings obvious to students—and involving students as interpreters and practitioners of these operations—is both theoretically and practically legitimate and important in the context of foreign language education. This includes, of course, the intercultural component at the same time as it works in the direction of content-based teaching and learning.

Lawrence Venuti's book *The Translator's Invisibility* (1995, p. 306; compare Venuti 1996) makes a similar argument:

> Translation is a process that involves looking for similarities between languages and cultures—particularly similar messages and formal techniques—but it does this only because it is constantly confronting dissimilarities. It can never and should never aim to remove these dissimilarities entirely. A translated text should be the site where a different culture emerges, where a reader gets a glimpse of a cultural other, and resistancy, a translation strategy based on an aesthetic of discontinuity, can best preserve that difference, that otherness, by reminding the reader of the gains and losses in the translation process and the unbridgeable gaps between cultures.

Conclusion

This chapter takes up a series of duplicitous—double—relationships that affect our ability to foster foreign language literacy in our students. I began by outlining the political contexts in which our teaching takes place. Whether others situate the foreign language philologies and pedagogies as *Orchideenfächer* is largely beyond our control. The metaphor's thrust is instructive, however. Its unidirectionality offers a negative paradigm for dealing with the other duplicities that the chapter addresses. Those duplicities, whose dual nature necessarily evoke our own ambivalences, can offer opportunities for learning. As Venuti points out, these opportunities require that we resist the temptation to create seeming identities, or even unidirectionalities, in the relation between tenor and vehicle, culture of translation *from* and culture of translation *into*. Preserving duplicity, as I have discussed it here in its logistical, pedagogical, and theoretical facets, can be a liberating exercise for ourselves and for our students. It should therefore come as no surprise that Venuti recommends Kafka as a writer of resistance and liberation.

In advocating the inclusion of translation in the teaching of foreign language literacy, and in asserting the efficacy of geminated courses, I am obviously not arguing for the reinstatement of the grammar-translation method. Nevertheless, it remains to be seen whether the senses of duplicity that I have developed here are applicable in other contexts. In particular, we need to discuss (1) whether the constellation that operates in the Kafka courses is "translatable" to other contexts; and (2) whether the peculiar combination of philology and liberal arts education that I have been advocating is effective from the perspective of foreign language pedagogy. If the answer is negative, then translation may indeed, as the Italian phrase goes *(traduttore traditore)*, constitute a form of duplicitous betrayal. If, however, we can answer in the affirmative, then translation will not be a traducer but an opportunity to practice, for ourselves and for and with our students, fundamental skills and acts of critical thinking and interpretation.

ACKNOWLEDGMENTS

I am indebted to Sandra Gerbrandt of York University for bibliographical assistance. The fact that this is a revised version of an oral presentation will not escape the reader; I have retained some of the stylistic features of the original paper.

References

Adelman, C. (1984). Language Study and the New Reform in General Education. In *Strategies for the Development of Foreign Language and Literature Programs,* edited by Claire Gaudiani et al., pp. 109–21. New York: Modern Language Association.

Corngold, S. (1973). *The Commentators' Despair: The Interpretation of Kafka's Metamorphosis.* Port Washington, N.Y.: National University Publications.

Godard, B. (1990). A (Re)Appropriation as Translation. *Canadian Theatre Review* 64 (fall): 22–31.

Grimm, J., and W. Grimm. (1984). Ungeheuer. *Deutsches Wörterbuch,* vol. 11, sec. III. 1936, facsimile reprint Munich: Deutscher Taschenbuch Verlag, vol. 24, col. 691–707.

Harman, M. (1996). Digging the Pit of Babel: Retranslating Franz Kafka's *Castle. New Literary History* 27: 291–311.

Kafka, F. (1983). *The Complete Stories.* Edited by Nahum Glatzer. New York: Schocken.

———. (1991). *The Blue Octavo Notebooks.* Edited by Max Brod. Translated by Ernst Kaiser and Eithne Wilkins. Cambridge, Mass.: Exact Change.

———. (1992). *Nachgelassene Schriften und Fragmente,* II. Edited by Jost Schillemeit. In *Franz Kafka: Schriften, Tagebücher, Briefe: Kritische Ausgabe.* Edited by Jürgen Born et al. Frankfurt: S. Fischer.

———. (1996). *Die Erzählungen und andere ausgewählte Prosa[: Originalfassung].* Edited by Roger Hermes. Fischer Taschenbücher, 13270. Frankfurt: Fischer Taschenbuchverlag.

Klier, J. D. (1986). *Russia Gathers Her Jews: The Origins of the Jewish Question in Russia, 1772–1825.* DeKalb: Northern Illinois University Press.

Rivera-Mills, S. V., and B. N. Gantt. (1999). From Linguistic Awareness to Cultural

Awareness: A Translation Framework for the Spanish Language Classroom. *Journal of Language for International Business (JOLIB)* 10(2): 1–13.

Venuti, L. (1995). *The Translator's Invisibility: A History of Translation.* Translation Studies. London: Routledge.

——. (1996). Translation and the Pedagogy of Literature. *College English* 58(3) (March): 327–44.

Webber, M. J. (1993). Reading as Resistance: An Integrated Approach to Advanced German. Paper presented at the Panel "Reading at the Advanced Level: Who? What? How?" Convention of the Modern Language Association of America, Toronto, Ontario (December 29).

——. (1995). The Metamorphosis of the Foreign Language Director, or: Waking up to Theory. In *Redefining the Boundaries of Foreign Language Study,* edited by Claire J. Kramsch, pp. 185–217. Issues in Language Program Direction. New York: Heinle & Heinle.

9

Ethics, Politics, and Advocacy in the Foreign Language Classroom

NICOLAS SHUMWAY

Ethics, Politics, Morality, Advocacy—these are big words that I could never define to my own satisfaction, and probably not to anyone else's. So rather than try to define them in any abstract sense, I would like to do what literary people and historians like me do best: I would like to tell some stories.

The first story—actually more an observation than a story—comes from *La Divina Commedia* of Dante. In the poem Dante is allowed a lengthy journey during which he observes the state of many individuals enduring the punishments of Hell, undergoing the healing and reconciliation of Purgatory, and experiencing the eventual joy of Paradise. In a recent conversation, Peter Hawkins, who has published a book on Dante and the Bible, pointed out something quite peculiar about the individuals in Hell: they are alone—physically, but also emotionally and spiritually (Hawkins 1999). They are incapable of talking about anything but themselves, and they cannot acknowledge other people. The message is a powerful one: Hell is utter obsession with oneself, the inability to take into account, much less imagine, another human being. When Dante arrives in Purgatory, we note something quite different: the people in Purgatory, although still far from perfect, come in pairs and groups. For Dante, then, Hell is total isolation, whereas reconciliation with God begins with the reconciliation of one human being with another.

So what does this have to do with language teaching and literacy? A great deal, I would suggest. As language teachers, we issue an invitation to our students and provide a mechanism for imagining others and thereby for escaping a particular aspect of Dante's vision of Hell. For in Dante we see the ethical failure of truncated individuals who are in Hell partly because they were obsessed with themselves. They made no room for other people, and to some degree, despite their self-obsession, they probably failed even to imagine themselves particularly well. For that reason, there is always an ethical component in our task as we address questions like the following: What do we teach? Whom do we choose to talk about? Whom do we include, and whom do we decide to erase or just leave out? And what do students learn about themselves in this conversation with other people and other cultures?

Roman Catholic theology has given us a memorable phrase in this regard when it teaches of "the dignity of the human person." A very similar phrase occurs in the opening sentence of the Universal Declaration of Human Rights, approved by all members of the United Nations in 1948 and one of that organization's charter documents. In that declaration we read: "the inherent dignity . . . of all members of the human family is the foundation of freedom, justice and peace in the world." Later in the same document we find the term again in the phrase "the United Nations have in the Charter reaffirmed their faith in fundamental human rights, in the dignity and worth of the human person and in the equal rights of men and women."

Before I go on, let me emphasize that the notion of the dignity of the human person is a premise. (In geometry it would be called an axiom.) It is not a conclusion, it is not the result of an argument, and it cannot be proven using logical or empirical methods. Nor is it subject to Fishy arguments that would relativize everything. It is, in short, a position that we choose to embrace because we choose to embrace it. And making that choice involves what the German theologian Karl Barth would call a leap of faith, unsupported by corroborating evidence.

But once we make that leap to respect the dignity of the human person, we immediately find ourselves in a complex, shifting world that I am calling politics. Respect implies a community of at least two, someone who respects and someone who is respected. As the etymology of the term *politics* suggests, politics is about the *polis*, about relationships within a given community. Politics can choose to be unethical by failing to account for the other. But it will always wrestle with ethical questions. Consequently, it is only within a political frame—that is, within the relations between individuals—that we can talk about respect for the dignity of the human person.

As language teachers providing mechanisms for imagining other people, much of what we teach involves politics, particularly as we endeavor to teach literature and culture. For example, in teaching about Spanish American history and culture, I usually begin the story of Spanish America with the story of the Spanish Reconquest, a movement in which Spanish Christians begin driving Moors and Jews southward and eventually decreeing the expulsion of all non-Christians from the Iberian peninsula. That impulse for expansion and Christianization did not stop at Spain's southern borders. Rather, it continued for three centuries into what we call the Americas. The Reconquest is, consequently, an essential starting point for understanding the mentality of the Spanish *conquistadores* and colonizers who implanted their culture in a new continent. To the degree that students know anything about these events, they have no trouble condemning the Reconquest as an ethical failure, what with its religious intolerance and ethnic cleansing. Moreover, if I give students the vocabulary, they have no trouble condemning those phenomena based on respect for the dignity of the human person. Easy, right?

But then we read sections from Spain's great epic poem of the Reconquest *El Cid*. Mixing literature with ethics always clouds things. What can seem blazingly clear in the abstract goes out of focus as soon as we start imagining such abstractions in the context of individual human experience. In a memorable essay titled "El primer Wells," Borges once remarked that a literary text is never a single object; rather, it is a focal point of myriad relationships, capable of an infinite and plastic ambiguity (Borges 1995, p. 137). For some, he says, it is the Apostle, for others it is a map of the world, for still others it is a mirror of the reader's face, and for most of us it is all of these things at once. As always, Borges chose his images well. Literature is like the Apostle, the divinely sent messenger, because we expect the literary text to tell us something transcendent. Even in the most secular societies, people still turn to art as a kind of surrogate religion, because in some sense the art object allows us to feel, if not religion, at least religious nostalgia. The literary text is also a map of the world, as it implants in our fancy images of people and places we could not imagine otherwise. And yes, literature is also a mirror, for often it is in dialogue with the product of someone else's imagination that we find the ability to imagine ourselves.

And all of this happens when we read *El Cid*. Whether they have seen the Charleton Heston film or not, the Cid is hard for most Americans to dislike. When the work begins, he is a man who has fallen into disgrace, a classic underdog, a kind of poor kid from the other side of tracks who blew his best chance at getting ahead. But with a lot of effort, he curries the favor of the rich and the powerful, shows himself to be a highly successful Rambo-style soldier, and becomes, perhaps, the first self-made man in literary history.

Now we can condemn what the Cid did, but can we imagine the Cid? Can we stop abstracting about the dignity of the human person long enough to try to really imagine him? And it is here that things get more complicated, for, although killing Moors, even with the alleged assistance of Saint James the Apostle, bothers people, the Cid is right up front about his motives: he wants to honor his religion, serve his king, and accrue a bit of property and personal glory for himself. God, country, and personal success are his motives. And they are motives that speak loudly and clearly to many of my students. Moreover, although we may regret his methods, did not the Cid simply want to raise his family in a Christian nation, where everyone spoke the same language? And how was he to know that three hundred years later the movement he assisted would culminate in the expulsion of the Jews and Moors, clearly one of the most shameful events in Spanish history?

Ethical ambiguities pile up even more in Spanish American culture courses when we start talking about the evangelization of the indigenous populations of Spanish America. As uncritical heirs to the notoriously anti-Catholic and anti-Spanish historiography of Anglo-America, my students are prepared to denounce the Spanish as gold-grubbing, virgin-raping, nature-destroying native killers. And I would quickly include myself among the many who lament the genocidal intolerance of the conquest and the ecological devastation wrought by imported crops and farm animals, not to mention illnesses against which the indigenous populations had no immunity. But here it is worthwhile to remember that the first task of ethics is not condemnation but imagination.

Take, for example, the Spanish missionaries. Can we imagine what they might have felt in their encounters with the native peoples? Let me try to reconstruct one of the scenes they might have seen. Human sacrifice—blood sacrifice—was a common practice in all of Meso-America. The Aztecs, for example, indulged in something called the War of Flowers in which they would capture enemies to be sacrificed. And these were not just the average sacrifice. The ideal was to extract the heart of the victim as it was still beating. Close your eyes a minute and visualize with me how the Aztec priest would bind the victim to a flat rock. He would then plunge a stone dagger into the victim's chest, scoop out the heart, and raise it with both hands above his head in such a way that the blood from the still-beating heart would stream down his arms, torso, and legs, until it wet the ground. Now, I seriously doubt that even the most politically correct among us could witness such a scene and then say to a neighbor, "Well, that's just their culture."

Condemning these practices and events is easy—especially at this distance. What is not easy is imagining the human beings who committed such actions. I cannot speak of what the Aztecs had on their minds, but of the Roman Catholic missionary priests we know a great deal, because they left us extensive writings—a literacy that we can try to penetrate. We know, for example, that they lived with incredible contradictions, for at the same time they condemned blood sacrifice among the American indigenous, they had no trouble accepting *autos-da-fe* in which the Inquisition burned heretics at the stake, events that were at least as horrific as the Aztec sacrifices. And we also know that as they lived with these contradictions, they also believed in the dignity of the human person, for they read it, preached it, and no doubt in many cases practiced it.

But can we really imagine them? Do we know what motivated men to abandon the safety of Spain and venture into uncharted lands inhabited by unknown and frequently hostile peoples in order to teach and maybe convert them to Christianity? Do we know what spurred successive generations of missionaries to continue in that holy errand, knowing full well that more than half their number would meet an early death from starvation, illness, or murder at the hand of the peoples they sought to save? And can we understand why some of them rose to great moral heights in trying to protect the Indians from other Spaniards?

What, for example, moved Father Antonio Montesinos to stand in his pulpit in 1511, only nine years after the founding of Hispaniola, now the Dominican Republic, and denounce his fellow Spaniards in the following terms?

> I am the voice crying in the wilderness. You are in mortal sin . . . for the cruelty and tyranny you use in dealing with these innocent peoples. . . . Tell me by what right or justice do you keep these Indians in such cruel and horrible servitude? . . . Are these not men? . . . Have they not rational souls? Are you not bound to love them as you love yourselves? Be certain that, in such a state as this, you can no more be saved than the Moors or Turks. (cited in Herring 1960, pp. 173–74)

The literacy Montesinos shared with his congregants might have made recognizable the reference to John the Baptist as the voice crying in the wilderness. Similarly, his congregation no doubt already would have heard Jesus' commandment about loving others as we love ourselves. And even if a few of his listeners missed those references, every self-respecting Spaniard of that time would have felt insulted at being compared to Moors and Turks. My question is this: What motivated Father Montesinos to denounce his faithful and virtually assure that he would be put on the next ship back to Spain?

And what would motivate his fellow Dominican, Bartolomé de las Casas, to devote his entire life to protecting the Indians from abuse at the hands of the Spaniards? Largely because of Father las Casas's bravery, the indigenous populations gained a place in the Spanish colonial polity—a place, I might add, that they lost after the wars of independence and that they have yet to regain. Now, we can rightly point out that their place in the polity was often observed more in the breach than in the fact, but it nonetheless existed and stands in sharp contrast to the fumbling and ultimately much more cruel practices of their English counterparts in North America.

As a language and literature teacher trying to put students in close contact with another culture, I see as one of my tasks that of imagining those remarkable people, in hopes that in those imaginings we might find the beginnings of ethical understanding. Only then can we try to see how they felt the ethical imperative of imagining the dignity of the human person as they dealt with the politics of their time, with the pressures of living in their communities.

Up to this point, I have talked about medieval heroes and sixteenth-century missionaries. Since these people lived centuries before our own time, it is relatively easy to consider abstract ethical questions in the context of their distant lives. Ethical questions are always clearer when the examples are not right in your face. But as participants in the affairs of our own time and as teachers of younger generations, we face issues not unlike those I have described, and these issues cannot but intrude in our classrooms. Consider some of the examples I have confronted as a teacher of Spanish literature.

Spanish is not only the language of Cervantes, Lorca, and Borges. It is also the language of children living their entire lives in the garbage dumps of Mexico City and finding in the leavings of other people all their food and all their clothing—and the occasional sellable item that allows them periodically to participate in the money economy. They can tell their stories in Spanish, and through Spanish we can try to imagine them, their lives, their dignity, and their negotiations with the political realities of their existence. Why not include in our courses Alma Guillermoprieto's "Letter from Mexico City," which concerns the tragic existence of these children?

Spanish is also the language of Argentina's *desaparecidos*, the disappeared whose numbers are sometimes estimated to be near 30,000. It was in Spanish that they were wrenched from their homes, tortured, and murdered. And it is in Spanish that their relatives pressure government officials to tell the truth about what happened in those awful years between 1976 and 1983. Should we not include, perhaps, excerpts from Jacobo Timmerman's moving testimony of his own experience as a "disappeared" in *Preso sin nombre, celda sin número?*

It is in Spanish that President Hugo Chávez of Venezuela has resurrected a kind of populist-leftist rhetoric that the triumphal neoliberalism of the early

1990s had pronounced dead. And it is in Spanish that he justifies making friends with outcasts such as Saddam Hussein and Fidel Castro, while the United States maintains an embarrassed silence because most of our imported oil comes from Venezuela. Should not our students perhaps hear some of his ideas in his own words, easily accessible on the Internet?

It is in Spanish that thousands of young Mexican girls leave their homes to flock to the U.S. border, where they earn meager wages to manufacture inexpensive goods for export to the United States, now imported without duty because of the transformations wrought by NAFTA. These are vulnerable women, often abused and raped by men who, in Spanish, resent the women's new-found independence and its challenge to male dominance—as is told in a beautiful book of testimonies called *La flor más bella de la maquiladora*, recently translated and published by the Teresa Lozano Long Institute of Latin American Studies, which it is my honor to direct, with the title *Beautiful Flowers of the Maquiladora*.

It is in Spanish that thousands of Mexicans cross illegally into the United States to subsidize with their labor and low wages the lifestyle we enjoy. It is in Spanish that they miss their families and each week send back to Mexico funds estimated in the tens of millions of dollars. And it is in Spanish that many of them utter their last words as they die because their *coyote* took their money and abandoned them in the Sonora Desert. Why not include in our language courses articles by Jorge Bustamante, a Mexican sociologist who on several occasions disguised himself as an immigrant laborer and then wrote about the harrowing experiences of what it is like to be in the United States as an illegal worker?

And finally, it is in Spanish that thousands of Hispanic immigrants to this country experience the challenges of assimilation, the pain of discrimination, and the not infrequent success that adds to the powerful immigration narratives that occupy such a prominent place in this country's collective imagination. Many texts tell this tale, perhaps none better than Gustavo Perez-Firmat's *Life on the Hyphen*.

This, of course, is a minuscule list, but it demonstrates that the study of Spanish offers many opportunities for imagining others by penetrating their codes of literacy. This list is also colored by politics, for there is not a single item on it that does not reflect the judgments that communities make in order to see or erase other people, to hear or remain deaf to their stories.

In some cases, the politics impinge directly on us. Throughout the United States, we all live better because undocumented Spanish-speaking laborers pick our vegetables, build our houses, make our clothes, and work in the kitchens of our restaurants, often under conditions no American citizen would accept and in constant fear of being apprehended by a U.S. government organization euphemistically called a Service. Moreover, it is not unusual to read news stories like that of the Los Angeles clothing manufacturer who regularly arranged for agents of the U.S. Immigration Service to raid his factory the day before payday. Similarly, the women who work in the border *maquiladoras* enter our houses daily through the goods they manufacture, thus benefiting us with their low wages and unhealthy living conditions.

In sum, choosing to teach their stories is an ethical choice, for we are asking ourselves and our students to imagine the lives of people who are often erased from public consciousness. And in imagining their lives, we must also imagine their humanity and their right to dignity. This choice is not only an ethical one, for it immediately involves us in politics. But unlike the politics of the Cid or of those sixteenth-century Spanish missionaries, we are players in these politics. Choosing to imagine those people—to penetrate their literacy—places them in our community, which in turn challenges us to take a stand. And taking a stand brings me to the third term in my title: advocacy.

We hear contradictory statements about advocacy. Right-wing pundits of varying sorts tell us we should teach values but not indoctrinate, but they are not very helpful in drawing the line between the two. Folks to the left are often no better when they preach a stultifying political correctness, better for stopping a conversation than for starting and maintaining one. Others say we should let the facts speak for themselves and then allow the students to choose whatever they want. The problem is that the facts never speak for themselves, for no understanding comes without interpretation. Moreover, by exercising our duty as teachers to choose certain topics rather than others, we have already become advocates of sorts.

I have no chirpy little formula for resolving the dilemma of, on one hand, advocating things I believe in while, on the other, creating an environment in which students feel free to disagree with me. I can, however, point out several moments in my teaching when students have disagreed with me in spectacularly effective ways—which leads me to believe that advocacy in an atmosphere that permits disagreement is not impossible. Let me tell you about two recent experiences.

In teaching Mexican history, one cannot ignore the fact that the United States, after occupying Mexico City, forced Mexico in 1848 to sign a treaty that ceded more than half its national territory to the United States. My students usually do not know about those events, although most of them can sing the verse in the Marine Hymn that memorializes the occasion in its reference to the Halls of Montezuma. The brazen imperialism of the U.S. invasion of Mexico led such eminent Americans as Abraham Lincoln, Ralph Waldo Emerson, and Mark Twain to condemn the war, thus contributing to the pressures that eventually led Congress to pay Mexico $17 million in guilt money for territories that had in fact never been for sale.

I tell this story as an advocate, wanting my students to question other examples of U.S. expansionism, including our government's meddlesome policies of more recent times and the truly frightening prospect of American military involvement in Colombia in the name of the war against drugs. You can therefore imagine my chagrin when a Mexican student raised his hand and said, "Of course the really bad thing about the outcome of the war is that the United States kept the part with all the paved roads."

It was a funny and no doubt flippant remark, but it also made a fundamental point that neoconservatives never tire of making, namely, that investment in an orderly society increases wealth and that such investment happened on one side of the border to a much greater degree than on the other. I immediately asked him if that justified the war, to which he replied with a Spanish proverb, "No hay bien que por mal no venga" ("No good thing comes but by way of evil"). Someday I want to write a book on how proverbs can abort productive discussion—but I stray from my subject.

My second example happened only last year when I included a section on the pan-Mayan movement, which is sweeping much of Guatemala and parts of southern Mexico and Honduras. To explain the significance of the movement, I spent a good deal of time on the history of how political elites, from the Spanish conquest forward, had fragmented the indigenous communities. I described how the United Fruit Company virtually owned Guatemala for much of the twentieth century. I also discussed how the Guatemalan military in the 1980s, with the support of several U.S. presidents, killed many thousands of Indians in the name of combating Communist guerrillas, whom the indigenous communities were allegedly supporting. And I described the attempts being made to forge a unified political movement, based in part on recent linguistic research that sought to create a written, pan-Mayan dialect that might help all indigenous peoples move toward a mutually comprehensible language.

And I got in lots of trouble. My primary accuser was an upperclass student from Guatemala who said she was tired of Americans like me who could only talk about the problems of Latin America and never bothered to give the point of view of the middle class, which was trying to modernize their country and to bring it into the world economy. And of course, she was right. Latin America is filled with thousands of decent, hard-working, middle-class people who never cease striving to improve their countries. Indeed, it is often because of them that we can tell the stories of the underclasses that I want to include. I was both delighted that these people were upset and delighted with their disagreements with me. But they made such good points that I also had to conclude that advocacy has its limits and that indoctrination just is not what it used to be and probably never was.

It appears that in this essay what I have mostly done is tell stories. From Dante, I concluded that ethical understanding begins with an attempt to imagine the other and that that notion is implicit in much of what we do as foreign language teachers. In stories about the Cid and two Dominican priests, I considered the similarity between the politics in old stories and the politics in our stories, and I reiterated my wonderment about what could make people like Antonio Montesinos and Bartolomé de las Casas defy the powers of their time on behalf of the Indians. I then gave examples of some of the stories that we might tell in our own Spanish language classrooms and suggested that Dante's injunction to imagine the other falls just as strongly on us as on his lost souls in Hell. I then suggested that in choosing what stories we teach, we cannot avoid politics. Nor can we avoid becoming advocates and taking sides. But I also told how my own experiences with advocacy often go awry, and blessedly so, since nothing could be worse than ending the dialogue or stopping the conversation.

And that is actually what I hope will happen with this essay: that it will prod us to remember that comparing literacies is an ethical endeavor; that it will help us remember that politics cannot be avoided; and that advocacy is part of what we are all about—even if it is highly unlikely that any of us will ever have the last word.

References

Borges, J. L. (1952). El Primer Wells. In *Otras inquisiciones,* pp. 103–6. Madrid: Alianza Editorial.

Guillermoprieto, A. (1990). Letter from Mexico City. *The New Yorker* 66 (Sept. 17): 93–104.

Hawkins, P. S. (1999). *Dante's Testament: Essays on Scriptural Imagination.* Stanford: Stanford University Press.

Herring, H. C. (1960). *A History of Latin America.* 2d ed. New York: Knopf.

Iglesias Prieto, N. V. (1985). *La flor más bella de la maquiladora: Historias de vida de la mujer obrera en Tijuana.* Mexico City: Secretaría de Educación Pública. *Beautiful Flowers of the Maquiladora.* Translated by Michael Stone. Austin: University of Texas Press, Institute of Latin American Studies.

Pérez Firmat, G. (1994). *Life on the Hyphen: The Cuban-American Way.* Austin, Tx: University of Texas Press.

Timerman, J. (1982) *Preso sin nombre, celda sin número.* Barcelona: Editorial Cid.

United Nations. General Assembly Resolution 217 A (III) of 10 December 1948. Universal Declaration of Human Rights ⟨http://www.un.org/Overview/rights.html⟩.

Contributors

Associate professor of French linguistics in the Department of French and Italian at the University of Texas at Austin, CARL BLYTH is also the current director of Technology, Literacy, and Culture, an interdisciplinary concentration in the College of Liberal Arts. He coordinates the Lower Division French language program and teaches courses in French linguistics, sociolinguistics, and applied linguistics. His research interests include discourse grammar, sociocultural theories of language learning, and instructional technology. In collaboration with departmental colleagues, he has completed several technology projects including an on-line reference grammar of French and an electronic textbook for first-year French called *Français interactif.* Currently, he is working on an edited volume for the series Issues in Language Program Direction titled *The Sociolinguistics of Foreign Language Classrooms: Contributions of Native, Near-native, and Non-native Speakers* (Boston: Heinle).

SILKE VON DER EMDE is associate professor of German studies at Vassar College. She has published articles on GDR literature, feminist theory, and German film and is currently completing a book on GDR author Irmtraud Morgner. She and her colleague Jeffrey Schneider have used MOOs extensively for collaborative language learning projects between students at Vassar College and other colleges and universities in the United States and Germany.

An associate professor of Slavic languages at Brown University, MASAKO

UEDA FIDLER is currently executive officer of the North American Association of Teachers of Czech and co-editor of its newsletter, *Czech Language News*. Her publications deal with Russian morphosyntax and comparative analysis of discourse strategies in Czech, Japanese, and Russian. She is working on the *Brown Czech Anthology*, a Web site project currently supported by the Consortium for Language Teaching and Learning.

Senior lecturer in the Section of Languages and Literatures at the Massachusetts Institute of Technology, GILBERTE FURSTENBERG is the principal author of the pioneering multimedia fiction *A la rencontre de Philippe* and of the interactive documentary *Dans un quartier de Paris*. Both of these programs have won many awards, including the Gold Medal in Interactive Video from Cinema and Industry (Los Angeles), the Mark of Excellence award from the International Interactive Communications Society (Washington, D.C.), and the Prix Special du Jury at the Innovalangues competition at Expolangues (Paris). Her current teaching and research focus on computer-based cross-cultural communication and understanding.

WILLIAM A. JOHNSON is assistant professor of classics at the University of Cincinnati. In the 1980s he was co-developer, with David W. Packard, of the Ibycus Scholarly Personal Computer, the first computer to allow the editing, search, and retrieval of ancient texts in a fully integrated desktop package, and one of the first two companies in the United States to market an application for CD-ROM technology. Since that time, he has returned to the academy, where he has written and lectured extensively on books, readers, and reading in the ancient and modern worlds. A study titled *Bookrolls and Scribes in Oxyrhynchus* is in press at the University of Toronto, and he is currently working on a book titled *Readers and Reading Culture in the Early Empire*.

RICHARD G. KERN is associate professor of French and director of the French language program at the University of California at Berkeley. He supervises graduate teaching assistants and teaches courses in French, applied linguistics, and foreign language pedagogy. His research interests include reading and writing in a foreign language and the use of networked computers to facilitate communicative language use. His most recent book, *Literacy and Language Teaching*, deals with the theory and practice of reading and writing in a foreign language. He also recently co-edited a collection of research studies with Mark Warschauer titled *Network-Based Language Learning: Concepts and Practice*.

PETER C. PATRIKIS is the founding executive director of the Consortium for Language Teaching and Learning, an assembly of ten private research institutions including Brown University, the University of Chicago, Columbia University, Cornell University, Dartmouth College, Harvard University, the Massachusetts Institute of Technology, the University of Pennsylvania, Princeton University, and Yale University. He has published and lectured widely in the United States and abroad on foreign language education, the place of computer technology in higher education, and general education.

JEFFREY SCHNEIDER is assistant professor of German studies at Vassar College. Together with Silke von der Emde, he has developed an on-line German-language MOO called MOOssiggang, which has been used successfully in a variety of courses at Vassar. In addition to ongoing research on technology in the foreign language curriculum, he is currently writing a book-length study of militarism, masculinity, and male sexuality in imperial Germany.

The Tomás Rivera Regents Professor of Spanish American Literature at the University of Texas at Austin, NICOLAS SHUMWAY is the director of the Teresa Lozano Long Institute of Latin American Studies. He has published extensively on Spanish American literature and cultural history and is also author of a successful first-year Spanish language textbook, *Español en Español*. His book *The Invention of Argentina* was selected by *The New York Times* as a notable book of the year. He is currently completing a book on the literature and thought of the nineteenth-century independence movements in Spanish America.

MARK TURNER is a distinguished professor at the University of Maryland, where he is a member of the department of English language and literature and the doctoral program in neuroscience and cognitive science. He has written articles and books on the nature of cognition and language. In 1996, the Académie française awarded him the Prix du Rayonnement de la langue et de la littérature françaises.

Associate director of the Canadian Centre for German and European Studies at York University (Toronto), MARK WEBBER teaches German and humanities. Co-author of *Für- und Widersprüche,* an advanced-level content-based textbook for German studies, he has also published on issues of nineteenth- and twentieth-century German literature, metaphor, curriculum design, and interculturality. He is program officer of the Ontario/Baden-Württemberg Student Exchange and co-director of the Canadian-German-Polish project "Learning from the Past—Teaching for the Future."

Index